THE ORGANIZED TEACHER TOOLKIT

THE ORGANIZED TEACHER TOOLKIT

Strategies for Managing Time, Classroom Space, and Boundaries

KRISTEN DONEGAN

For Liv and Kai—who remind me that joy lives in the little moments, that presence is the truest gift, and that everything is, indeed, figureoutable. Being your mama is the best part of my life.

And to teachers everywhere—may this book remind you that rest is not a reward, joy is not indulgent, and you are doing better than you think.

Contents

Hey There, I'm Kristen, and I Was a Workaholic

Ever since I was a little girl I wanted to be a teacher. I was that kid who would dig out dried out Expo markers and unused copies from my teacher's trash can so that I could play school at home for hours. I can't tell you how hard I tried to even create my own overhead projector with my parents' old slide projector! Being a teacher was the only thing I ever wanted to do, so you can imagine my excitement when I finally had my very own classroom . . . with a working overhead projector.

I didn't go into teaching blindly. Everyone always said that teachers were underpaid and worked long hours, so I expected that. But I had no idea how this reality would truly impact my life both in and out of the classroom.

I made a really big mistake for the first half of my teaching career and maybe you're making this mistake too.

Early on in my teaching career, I believed in order to be effective, productive, and a really good teacher, I had to stay late and bring work home because there just weren't enough hours in the day.

It seemed like the only way I could create engaging lessons that met the needs of all of my students, organize and manage differentiated centers, document behavior, find missing work, catch up on grading, respond to one million emails, attend meetings, and everything else that was demanded of me, was to work at nights and on most weekends because it was the only way I could make my to-do list any smaller.

For the first few years, I really loved spending most of my free time on school stuff. I was just so happy to finally have my own classroom; I loved spending time there and trying to come up with solutions to the everyday problems I was facing as a teacher. And this was all before Pinterest and Teachers Pay Teachers, so I spent hours and hours reinventing the wheel.

I thought I was fine working 70 hours per week and thought it was completely normal because when I looked around my school, it's what so many other teachers (even the veterans) were doing. Plus, I was a brand new teacher and was starting with pretty much nothing so long hours were just part of the territory—right?

Can you relate to this at all?

My friends and family became used to me bringing stacks of grading on vacation or missing out on family time while on that very same vacation because I was so exhausted that I spent the majority of my time catching up on sleep. One aunt used to give me such a hard time and would say, "You can sleep when you're dead!" Clearly, she wasn't a teacher and just didn't understand how much I gave of myself that I'd often be so exhausted when I had any sort of down time. I missed out on a lot of valuable family time that I'll never get back.

I just thought, "I guess this is just part of teaching." I thought I was fine with this busy schedule, but I wasn't. I went on this way for the first seven years in the classroom because I just couldn't figure out how to get everything done. And whenever I felt like I was getting close to completing my to-do list, more would get added to it!

After being 1 of the 400 tenured teachers laid off in my district in Southern California due to budget cuts the same year I earned my Masters and Reading Specialist certificate, I had a phone interview for a first grade position in Hawaii.

I remember being so proud of my answer at the time but cringe when I recall it because it was so toxic. The principal asked me what was something I could improve as a teacher, or something along those lines. My mom always taught me to reframe a negative quality into a positive one so I proudly said, "Most nights, I stay too late at school creating lessons and working in my classroom." At the time, although this answer was true, I thought it portrayed how dedicated I was but now realize I lacked boundaries and systems in my classroom so that I could also have a life outside of

x

Hey There, I'm Kristen, and I Was a Workaholic

being a teacher. I did however get that position and moved to Hawaii two weeks later with a few suitcases and two boxes.

The breaking point for me came a few years later when I was hired to teach a ½ combo the year Common Core was being implemented at a school 50 miles away the day before school started. Can you believe it? That was one of the hardest years in my 13 years as a teacher. That was the year that teaching put me in the hospital. No matter how many hours I stayed after school and on the weekends, I was barely getting by.

That year, I was always the last teacher out of the parking lot, leaving when it was pitch-black outside, picking up greasy fast food on my hour-drive home. And then I'd walk in the door and change into my jammies, plop on the couch, and catch up on lesson-planning or grading with my laptop and my favorite reality show.

I was also teaching an intervention class after school and led several committees to help teachers implement best teaching practices, so by the time I finally got to work on actual things I needed for my own classroom, school had already been out for a few hours. After school, and if we're being honest, when I was watching TV at night or taking a shower in the morning, I was constantly thinking about my teacher list that never got smaller! I wished more than anything that I could just shut off my teacher-brain, but I didn't know how! So much was on my plate that I had trouble ever getting caught up, so working long hours seemed like the only way to be able to have every-thing I needed to actually teach!

No matter how many hours I stayed after school and on the weekends, I was barely getting by.

I found myself planning for my math lesson minutes before my students were about to walk back in from lunch and making last-minute copies in my classroom. I would've gone on this way because I had no idea how to get everything done. The newness and excitement had worn off by this point, and I was drowning and running on adrenaline and my new coffee habit I picked up that year.

I got a massive wake-up call one evening when I had a panic attack and couldn't catch my breath. I don't know if you've ever experienced one before but it was really scary because I was hyperventilating and couldn't breathe. When I was laying in the

Hey There, I'm Kristen, and I Was a Workaholic

ER, they told me I needed to make some changes in my life, immediately. That was the moment I realized that being a workaholic (although praised by my colleagues and principal) had major repercussions on my life and my health.

And maybe you're like I was then. Maybe you're having trouble getting everything done as a teacher and it's taking away from the things you truly love like precious time with your family, working out, and just being able to relax. Maybe you're having trouble getting everything done, especially with all the changes in education you've experienced the last few years.

I was unable to make time for the other things outside of the classroom that really mattered to me. I had lost a big chunk of myself and no longer made time for the things I loved like surfing, running, and happy hour with friends because I accidentally let teaching consume me.

What types of things are you unable to make time for anymore because teaching got in the way?

And if you've given up a lot, chances are you've also given so much to your students that you barely have any time for the people in your life who matter most.

In the hospital, I realized that no matter what, I needed to find a way to spend less time on school stuff and more time on the things that made me happy and healthy. I needed a system to make better use of my time while still protecting it. That's the year when The Organized Teacher System was created. It was my solution to spending less time on school stuff and bringing some much-needed balance back to my life.

I became obsessed with creating different systems and routines in my classroom that would ensure that our classroom was a well-oiled machine so that I was no longer working at all hours of the night! I created systems to pass out and collect student work easily, effective center organization that took little time to set up, systems for students to work independently without interrupting our small reading groups, systems to finally lesson efficiently and being completely prepped for the following week by Thursday, ways to grade faster AND get student work back the same week, and so much more.

Hey There, I'm Kristen, and I Was a Workaholic

As I became obsessed with finding the very best solutions to common classroom problems I was experiencing that you probably are as well, I began to notice that my students knew exactly what to do. Research shows that when students have consistent routines, behaviors decrease. This meant that I was no longer repeating myself all day, which made me a happier teacher. It also allowed me to be more present during teaching without stressing that we have to rush through this lesson because we're behind. I was able to leave school on time without bringing work home. I got my nights and weekends back and if I decided to work longer, it wasn't because I was guilted into doing so, it was because I wanted to, not because I was "voluntold" to do so!

I finally pulled together everything that was actually helping me stay organized, protect my time, and feel more in control at school. I bundled it all into a simple, proven approach that I now teach to elementary teachers all over the country. It's called **The Organized Teacher System**, and thousands of K–5 teachers inside The Organized Teacher Club are already using it to leave school prepared *and* get home on time.

Throughout this book, you'll get a look at the core pieces of this system—**Boundaries, Time Management, Clutter-Free Spaces, and Sustainable Organization Systems**—so you can use what works for you and create your own version that fits your life and your classroom. I'm doing this because I wholeheartedly believe that this resource should be in every credential program, new teacher program, and district professional development (PD) so that teachers like you don't have to continue to struggle. You deserve to be the best version of yourself both in and out of the classroom, and you opening up this book today speaks volumes about who you are. This is the stuff you actually need and truly deserve so you can live your best life both in and out of the classroom.

Task: Make a list of 3–5 things that you wish you had more time to do outside of the classroom.

exxxistence/
Adobe Stock Photo

Hey There, I'm Kristen, and I Was a Workaholic

Downloadable Materials

Scan the QR code to access the following organization and time-saving resources mentioned throughout the book:

Chapter 3

- Sample PLC Meeting Agenda

- Decision-Making Flow Map for Saying "No"

Chapter 4

- "I'm Busy" Note

Chapter 6

- Keep/Toss/Action Decluttering Labels

- Decision-Making Flow Map for Decluttering

- File Folder Dividers

Chapter 9

- Digital Planning Template

- Auto-Populating Weekly Schedule

Chapter 10

- Auto-Populating Grading List

- Editable Rubric

Chapter 11

- Important Stuff Label

- Turn-In Label

- Editable Absent Note

- Unfinished Work Note

- Editable Sub Plans Template

Scan to get this download

Hey There, I'm Kristen, and I Was a Workaholic

Chapter 1

The Truth About Teaching No One Is Talking About

If it were as simple as me sharing proven organization systems with you so that you could leave school prepared more often, you'd already be doing it. But there's a reason why you may find yourself in this never-ending cycle no matter if you're new to teaching or have been teaching for 20 years. Perhaps there are several other factors that contribute to teaching being all-consuming and it's important to examine them.

I'm all about keeping it real and before we begin, I have to take a moment to acknowledge something that often gets overlooked—the challenges you face as a teacher are real. They're not just complaints or things you should "get over" with more resilience or better time management. They are legitimate, heavy, and often overwhelming. You're not imagining the pressure, the exhaustion, or the weight of responsibilities that seem to grow by the day. You're carrying a load that, truthfully, was never meant to be carried by one person alone.

If you've ever felt like you're drowning under unrealistic expectations, like no matter how hard you work it's never enough, or like you're constantly being pulled in a thousand directions, you're not alone. I see that, and more importantly, I want *you* to recognize that those feelings don't come from weakness or lack of dedication. They come from a system that asks too much and gives too little in return. And yet, here you are, showing up every single day for your students, giving them your energy, your patience, and your heart. It says a lot about who you are as a human.

You deserve to feel supported. You deserve to leave school on time without carrying guilt home with you. And you deserve a career that allows you to thrive, not just survive. I want you to know that everything you're feeling is valid and this book isn't about brushing past those struggles with quick fixes. It's about facing those challenges head-on, recognizing what's within your control, and helping you build the boundaries, systems, and mindset you need to protect your well-being. You are not the problem, the system is. But there are ways to reclaim your time, energy, and joy within that system. And that's what I'm here to help you do.

The challenges you're facing in the classroom aren't just personal struggles, they're widespread, systemic issues backed by research. If you feel like the demands of teaching have become more intense in recent years, you're not alone. Studies continue to show that teachers across the country are dealing with increasing stress, larger workloads, and declining job satisfaction. Let's look at the five unspoken roles that are facing educators like you and then look at what you can control. These rules aren't about helping you be a better teacher, they're about keeping a broken system running.

When you think about your school, are there unspoken rules that exist?

The unspoken rules built into school culture often mirror and strengthen the limiting beliefs teachers internalize. Together, they create an invisible framework that keep you stuck in old patterns that make it hard to leave school at school or why you're in your working in your classroom while it's dark outside, convinced there's always just one more thing to finish.

You know the ones that you follow because it's just how your school runs. Unspoken rules in education don't exist by accident. In fact, they've developed over time as a way to keep schools running despite systemic challenges. Schools are often underfunded, resources are stretched thin, and there simply aren't enough hours in the day for everything that needs to get done. In response, these unspoken expectations have formed, encouraging teachers like you to go above and beyond to fill in the gaps. While they may have been created with good intentions—helping students, maintaining a strong school culture, or fostering teamwork—they can quickly become unhealthy when they lead to burnout, overwhelm, and a sense that teachers must constantly give more to be seen as dedicated.

The tricky part is that these rules are woven into the culture of schools passed down by well-meaning colleagues and reinforced in subtle (and not-so-subtle) ways. They're rarely stated outright, making them difficult to recognize and even harder to challenge. You're not told that you have to stay late, but if you leave at your contracted time, you might feel like you're not working hard enough or you may get glances from your coworkers, right? Or you may even be the one giving sideways glances when that one teacher always leaves at the bell. No one requires you to buy supplies for your classroom, but when something is missing, there's an unspoken expectation that you'll figure it out. You aren't forced to take on extra responsibilities, but when you decline, you might be met with comments like, *"We just really need a team player."* These messages can make it feel like saying no is letting your students or your colleagues down, even when the expectations themselves are unrealistic.

The reality is, even the most organized and hardworking teachers can't do it all because the system wasn't designed for one person to carry this much alone and I truly want you to know that. A 2024 RAND Corporation study[1] found that teachers work, on average, nine hours more per week than professionals in other fields, yet they report higher levels of stress and lower job satisfaction. This makes sense according to the 2024 State of Schools Report,[2] which states that 39% of teachers experience burnout very often or always.

Does this number seem accurate?

That doesn't mean administrators or district leaders are intentionally setting you up for burnout. Often, they're navigating their own pressures, making the best decisions they can within the constraints they're given. But if you're expected to take on more and more without the time, compensation, or resources to do it well, the system itself needs to be reexamined. I'm not here to place blame; I'm here to be real with you. The more you understand these unspoken rules and limiting beliefs you carry, the more you can make intentional choices about how you show up in your work. You get to decide what is sustainable for *you*. And that starts with recognizing that constantly going above and beyond shouldn't be the expectation, it should be the exception.

---

[1] "Teachers Report Worse Pay and Well-Being Compared to Similar Working Population," https://www.rand.org/news/press/2024/06/18.html.

[2] https://www.gallup.com/education/608843/state-of-schools-report-2024.aspx.

The Truth About Teaching No One Is Talking About

The reality is, you can be an incredible teacher *and* set boundaries. You can care deeply about your students *and* protect your own time and energy. Let's break them down so you can start making choices that serve *you*, not just the system.

Unspoken Rule #1: "Good Teachers Stay Late and Bring Work Home."

You've probably felt it—that pressure to keep working long after the school day ends. Maybe you've even told yourself that staying late or working through the weekend is just what *good* teachers do. If you've ever looked at your to-do list and thought, *There is no way I'm getting all of this done today,* you're not alone. The sheer volume of work expected of teachers is completely unrealistic. Teaching isn't just about delivering lessons—it's about planning, grading, managing behavior, tracking data, responding to emails, meeting with parents, attending professional development, differentiating instruction, filling out paperwork, supervising students, and somehow squeezing in time to eat and use the restroom. And that's *just* during the school day.

It's no surprise that many teachers end up taking work home every night or staying late just to catch up. I'll never forget what one of my amazing professors, Kathy Murphy at Cal State Fullerton, told our class during our credential program. She said, "The #1 reason teachers leave the profession within the first five years is because of all of the administrative paperwork" and that always stuck with me. A report by The American Federation of Teachers in 2022[3] found that administrative burdens are one of the biggest contributors to teacher stress and burnout because teachers are increasingly required to handle extensive data collection and reporting tasks, which often interfere with their primary teaching responsibilities. The report emphasizes that such administrative demands can lead to significant stress and detract from instructional time. Things like excessive documentation, unrealistic lesson plan requirements, and constantly changing policies pull your focus away from what actually matters—teaching and

---

[3] "Here Today, Gone Tomorrow? What America Must Do to Attract and Retain the Educators and School Staff Our Students Need," https://www.aft.org/sites/default/files/media/2022/taskforcereport0722.pdf.

supporting students. Instead of giving you more time to plan or collaborate, schools often pile on more paperwork, more data tracking, and more tasks that don't actually improve student outcomes.

But here's the reality: working longer hours doesn't make you a better teacher. It just makes you more exhausted. The best teachers aren't the ones who sacrifice their entire lives for the job, they're the ones who show up refreshed, prepared, and able to give their best *because* they've set boundaries around their time.

There's a deeply ingrained idea that teaching is a job that never really ends and that if you truly care about your students, you'll spend as much time as necessary planning, grading, and preparing. While flexibility is important, this expectation often leads to burnout, with teachers feeling guilty for setting boundaries around their time. The reality is that great teaching isn't about how many hours you work, it's about how effectively you use your time, among many other things. I'm curious, can't not-so-good teachers stay late and bring work home as well? Schools that recognize this and build in realistic planning and collaboration time help teachers maintain both effectiveness and longevity in the profession. The amount of time you put into teaching doesn't determine how effective you are.

Unspoken Rule #2: "Good Teachers Say 'Yes' to Extra Responsibilities."

Whether it's joining a committee that you're volun-told to run, running an after-school program, or picking up extra duties, there's an expectation that teachers should always *do more*. And while being a team player is great, saying yes to everything just isn't sustainable.

Do you ever do this?

I fell into the trap of saying yes to extra duties because I wanted to be liked, I wanted to be helpful, and I didn't want to burden my team. I didn't realize that by saying yes to everyone else, I was actually saying no to me. You don't have to prove your dedication by overloading yourself. Protect your time. Choose the things that energize you, not the ones that drain you. And remember: just because you *can* do something doesn't mean you *have to*. I always tell teachers

The Truth About Teaching No One Is Talking About

that when making decisions, if it's not a heck yes, then it's a no. There's nothing worse than saying yes to something that you end up resenting or just don't have capacity for.

Unspoken Rule #3: "It's for the Kids."

This is the guilt trip that gets teachers every time. Anytime you hesitate to take on something extra, you hear it: *"It's for the kids."* And yes, we're all here for the kids. It's why you got into the profession in the first place. But that doesn't mean you have to give everything you have so that you have nothing left to give when you get home.

Let's be real—every year, it feels like more is added to your plate, but the support you actually need never seems to follow. Your classroom is more complex than ever, with diverse student needs, new curriculum demands, challenging behaviors, and technology that's supposed to make things easier. But instead of getting the time, training, and resources to actually implement these changes, you're often left to figure it out on your own. And when that support isn't there, what's meant to *help* you ends up just making your job harder.

According to the Pew Research Center,[4] "the vast majority of teachers say there's not enough time in the workday to accomplish all that's expected of them." How often do you feel the same way? "Some 84% say they don't have enough time during their regular work hours to do tasks like grading, lesson planning, paperwork and answering emails." There's a lack of support across the board. You've probably spent thousands of dollars of your own money to purchase classroom supplies because your school's budget doesn't cover even the basics. Maybe you've sat through professional development that had *nothing* to do with what you actually need. Maybe you've asked for instructional support but were told, *"We just don't have the resources or funding."* Or maybe you've received amazing professional development based on the latest research and once you figure out how to take this back to your classroom, you find out that there's no funding to purchase the tools and materials you need to actually implement

---

[4] https://www.pewresearch.org/social-trends/2024/04/04/how-teachers-manage-their-workload/.

The Organized Teacher Toolkit

these best practices. It's frustrating, because you *want* to do right by your students, but the system isn't giving you what you need to do your job *within* the very limited time you're given.

A system that depends on teachers overworking themselves *isn't actually putting kids first*—because burned-out teachers don't serve students well. Taking care of yourself isn't selfish. It's necessary. A helpful way to reframe this unspoken rule is to change it to, "It's for the kids and what I have capacity for."

How does this reframe feel?

You are a professional. You deserve a career that respects both your passion and your well-being. And the more we shift this mindset individually and collectively, the better chance we have of making teaching a profession where great educators *want* to stay.

> Because a system that depends on teacher burnout isn't sustainable. But one that values teachers as whole people? That's the system our students *and* educators truly deserve.

Unspoken Rule #4: "We are Family."

You hear this phrase all the time in schools—*"We're a family here."* And while it sounds nice, it's often used to justify asking teachers to give more than they should. How many times have you taken on extra responsibilities because of this unspoken rule? A healthy workplace should have teamwork, collaboration, and support, but it should *not* expect you to work unpaid hours, say yes to everything, or blur the lines between your professional and personal life in the name of "family." And being guilted into extra work seems like manipulation, right? Families are built on unconditional love (in a perfect world) and workplaces are built on contracts and expectations. You can care about your colleagues and your students *without* being expected to sacrifice yourself, or your actual family, for the job.

The Truth About Teaching No One Is Talking About

Unspoken Rule #5: "Be Flexible and Don't Push Back."

Flexibility is an important part of teaching because things change, and you have to adapt and you most likely do it all day long! But in many schools, *"be flexible"* doesn't just mean adjusting to changes, it means accepting whatever happens without question. There's an unspoken expectation that teachers should go along with last-minute schedule shifts, new initiatives with no training, or added responsibilities *without pushing back*. If you question these changes or advocate for yourself, you might be labeled as "negative" or "not a team player."

This unspoken rule is especially harmful because it discourages teachers from speaking up about real issues. You might hesitate to ask for clarity on a new policy, express concerns about an unrealistic expectation, or even just say, *"I can't take on more right now."* But constantly going along with every change without question doesn't make you a better teacher; it just makes you more exhausted and maybe even a little resentful. Schools function best when teachers are empowered to provide feedback and advocate for what they need to do their jobs effectively. I know you want your voice to be heard and respected. Flexibility should be about collaboration and problem-solving, not about staying silent and accepting whatever is thrown your way.

If you've ever thought about leaving teaching or if you know colleagues who have, you're not alone. The 2026 State of California's Public Schools found that 40% of TK–12th grade teachers are considering leaving education in the next few years.[5] These numbers aren't just statistics; they represent real teachers who started their careers full of passion but found themselves burned out, disillusioned, or unable to sustain the workload. The teaching profession is facing a major crisis. It's hard to retain qualified teachers as teachers are leaving the profession at an alarming rate. According to data

---

[5] California Teachers Association, *The State of California Public Schools*, 2026, https://www.cta .org/document/the-state-of-ca-public-schools.

from the Bureau of Labor Statistics,[6,7] around 300,000 public school teachers and other related staff left the education field from February 2020–May 2022. This large exodus was approximately 3% of that workforce, reaching 10% nationally.

So why are so many teachers leaving? One of the biggest reasons is the increasing workload without additional support or compensation. Teachers today are not just educators, they're expected to be curriculum developers, intervention specialists, social-emotional coaches, tech support, and paperwork processors. While teachers have always worn multiple hats, the demands have only grown in recent years, especially with the rise of new policies, initiatives, and accountability measures. And yet, salaries have barely kept up with inflation, and support systems in schools are often lacking. Teachers are being asked to do more while being given less. Are you nodding your head "yes?"

Another major factor is the lack of respect and autonomy in the profession. Many teachers feel micromanaged by policies that don't take classroom realities into account. Curriculum mandates, standardized testing pressures, and rigid instructional requirements can make even experienced educators feel like they have little control over their own teaching. Instead of being trusted as professionals, teachers are often treated as if they need constant oversight and evaluation. When teachers don't feel respected or valued, it becomes harder to stay in a profession that constantly demands more without recognizing the expertise and dedication that educators bring to the table, right? And there's also the lack of respect from the community and the "brave" online keyboard warriors who haven't stepped inside a classroom to actually see what is truly going on. It can leave you feeling pretty defeated some days because you are doing your very best.

School culture also plays a huge role in whether teachers stay or leave. A supportive administration, strong colleague relationships, and a healthy work environment can make even a challenging job feel sustainable. But when teachers feel isolated, overworked, or unsupported, burnout happens fast. Many educators report that when they've expressed concerns about workload, student behavior, or the need for better resources, they're met with responses like, *"Just be flexible,"* or *"That's just the way it is."*

---

[6]"School's Out for Summer and Many Teachers Are Calling It Quits," *Wall Street Journal,* https://www.wsj.com/articles/schools-out-for-summer-and-many-teachers-are-calling-it-quits-11655732689.

[7]RAND Survey, https://www.rand.org/pubs/research_reports/RRA956-14.html.

The Truth About Teaching No One Is Talking About

This kind of dismissive culture pushes teachers out the door faster than almost anything else. I excelled when I taught at schools where I felt incredibly supported and my happiness suffered at schools that were toxic and harmful until I was able to transfer to a better environment.

And of course, mental health and work–life balance are major contributors to teacher turnover. The expectation that teachers will work beyond their contracted hours grading at night, planning on weekends, and answering emails at all hours makes it nearly impossible to maintain a personal life. Teachers often leave not because they don't love teaching, but because the job demands more than they can give while still having time for their families, health, and well-being.

If you've ever considered walking away from teaching, I want you to know that it doesn't mean you're not dedicated or strong enough. The system has been structured in a way that makes it difficult to stay long-term without sacrificing yourself. But the solution isn't just about your personal resilience, it's about setting boundaries, advocating for better working conditions, and creating a culture where teachers can thrive instead of just surviving. Because while some challenges are beyond our control, there *are* ways to make teaching sustainable. And you deserve to be in this profession *without* burning out in the process.

My hope is that after hearing these unspoken rules, some of which you may have experienced in your school, you begin to see that there are many factors that prevent you from leaving school on time more often that have nothing to do with what is happening in your actual classroom. I also want to acknowledge the challenges you face and so much that is out of your control and I know how very real that is for you. I experienced the same feelings and frustrations during the first seven years in the classroom until I created systems that made it possible to finally be prepared, calm, and excited to teach because I wasn't up late planning the night before or making copies five minutes before my math lesson. Here's the thing you need to know. The education system isn't changing anytime soon, but you can and that's pretty powerful.

The system wasn't designed to make this job manageable. But that doesn't mean you have to give in to the pressure to overwork yourself just to *prove* that you're a good teacher.

And yet, many teachers feel like they have no choice. Why? Because beyond the structural challenges, there's also a set of *deeply ingrained beliefs* that keep teachers

The Organized Teacher Toolkit

stuck in a cycle of overworking, overcommitting, and feeling like no matter what they do, it's never enough. These beliefs aren't always taught outright, but they show up in unspoken expectations, subtle pressures from colleagues and administrators, and even our own self-doubt. I struggled with them for many years.

You've probably felt it yourself, that moment when you see a colleague's car still in the parking lot long after school is over and wonder, *Should I be staying later too?* Or the guilt that creeps in when you leave on time, as if walking out the door means you're not as dedicated as the teachers who work into the evening. Or you may roll your eyes when the teacher down the hall leaves at dismissal again while you're still stuck trying to plan for the rest of the week. We've been conditioned to believe that being the last (or first) car in the parking lot *means something* about our worth as teachers. But here's the truth: it doesn't. *The amount of time you spend working doesn't define your teaching ability.* Please read that again!

What Actually Makes a Good Teacher? (Hint: It's Someone Who's Getting Their Needs Met)

We agree that a "good teacher" isn't the one who stays the latest, says yes to everything, never complains, and sacrifices their personal life for their students, right? While that version has been celebrated for years, times are changing because we know that it's just not sustainable, especially in today's education climate.

A good teacher is someone who's clear on their priorities and creates a classroom rooted in consistency, care, and high expectations. They build relationships, plan with purpose, and use their time intentionally. But just as importantly, a good teacher takes care of themselves. They set boundaries, protect their planning time, and recognize that their job is important, but so is their well-being. When teachers are rested, supported, and not running on empty, *that's* when their students benefit the most. You can't pour into your students if you're constantly running on fumes.

Inside The Organized Teacher Club, we talk a lot about this: a good teacher is someone who is getting their needs met. That might look different from teacher to teacher, but the bottom line is this: when you feel calm, confident, and in control of your time, you show up differently. You're more present and more patient. You're

The Truth About Teaching No One Is Talking About

more *you*. Think of how you show up on the days you know you get to attend your favorite work out class or you have plans with family or friends after school. Or how you show up after a weekend of rest or going away on a trip. That version of you—the one who's balanced, energized, and supported—is the one your students (and your family) need most. Not the burnt-out, overworked version that's constantly being sold as "what a good teacher does." You deserve better. And your students do, too. And so does your family.

A good teacher might look like the one who decides to stop grading every single assignment in detail and instead starts using quick checks for understanding, so she can spend her evenings having dinner with her family instead of glued to a stack of papers. Or the teacher who sets a timer for 45 minutes during her planning period, focuses on one task at a time, and actually walks out the door near contract time guilt-free. She's not cutting corners, she's cutting out the noise so she can focus on what matters most. That's not laziness. That's being intentional.

It might be the teacher who no longer volunteers for every school event or committee, even though she used to say yes to everything. Now, she asks herself, *"Is this aligned with my priorities and capacity right now?"* before responding. Maybe she's decided not to run the after-school club this year (even though she's done it for the last five) because she's caring for an aging parent or trying to be more present at home with her newborn. That doesn't make her less dedicated. That makes her wise. She knows that by saying no to some things, she's protecting her ability to give her best to the things she's already committed to.

Or it might be the teacher who shows up in the morning with a full cup of coffee and a clear plan, not because she stayed up until midnight prepping, but because she finally created a system that works so she's planned ahead of time. She's using the copy bin system, she's batching her lesson plans weekly, and she's using her planning time for actual planning, not random last-minute tasks. Her room might not be perfectly decorated or color-coded, but it runs smoothly, her students are engaged, and she leaves school most days without taking work home. And when she stays later, it's because she wants to. That's what it looks like to have your needs met and still do your job well.

The Organized Teacher Toolkit

These are the teachers who are redefining what it means to be "good." Not the martyrs but the intentional, boundary-setting, joy-protecting professionals who are in this for the long haul. And you can be one of them. And now that you've made it this far, the next chapter is where we get into the heart of this book. I'll show you exactly how to start by sharing practical steps that will help you leave school prepared more often by using The Organized Teacher System.

Task: Which unspoken rule resonates with you the most and why?

exxxistence/
Adobe Stock Photo

Chapter 2

How to Leave School Completely Prepared Without Working Nights and Weekends

If you're like most teachers, you probably spend most afternoons trying to complete your to-do list and get planned for the next day, hoping that if you just stay a little longer, things will finally feel under control. But what often happens is that once the bell rings, you're often sitting at your desk unsure where to even start first. And the next thing you know, it's dark out and you're the last car in the parking lot . . . again. The problem isn't that you're doing it wrong, it's that you're trying to leave school prepared and on time without a proven system that truly supports you. It's the #1 thing organized teachers are using right now to not only make teaching sustainable, but enjoyable as well, and it's absolutely essential so that they don't have to continue choosing between school and home. They get to be a well-rounded teacher who not only crushes it at school, but gets to come home and have hobbies and be super-present with their family. You can have that too. If you're one of the teachers without a successful system in place yet, it's okay and it's not your fault. You haven't been taught a better way until now, so let's change all that, okay?

I'm going to teach you that in this book, so you can transform the way you're being as a teacher. I want you to love your life both in and out of the classroom again. I'm here to tell you: it's absolutely possible. I've seen this with the thousands of teachers I've been lucky enough to work with. They were once where you are, and they've just put simple yet powerful systems in place that make their day easier. They are happier and less stressed because they aren't feeling like they are sinking. My goal is to take you from the overwhelmed teacher to the completely opposite.

What is that for you?

You may be wondering what this organization system is? **The Organized Teacher System is a simple, sustainable framework or system that helps K–5 teachers leave school prepared and on time—without being the last car in the parking lot.** It streamlines the "other stuff" teachers juggle every day by combining time management, boundaries, clutter-free spaces, and organization systems into one cohesive approach. **When teachers use it, they spend less time scrambling and more time teaching well, living well, and actually enjoying both.** How does that sound?

In the chapters ahead, you're going to learn about this proven system as you discover how to set boundaries that stick, manage your time with intention, create a clutter-free classroom you can actually think in, and build simple organization systems that help you leave school prepared more often.

By the end of this book, **you'll have a clear plan for getting the right things done during the school day—without staying late, sacrificing your home life, or running on fumes.** You'll know exactly how to prevent overwhelm before it starts, how to make decisions with confidence, and how to reclaim the joy and energy that make you a better teacher and a happier human.

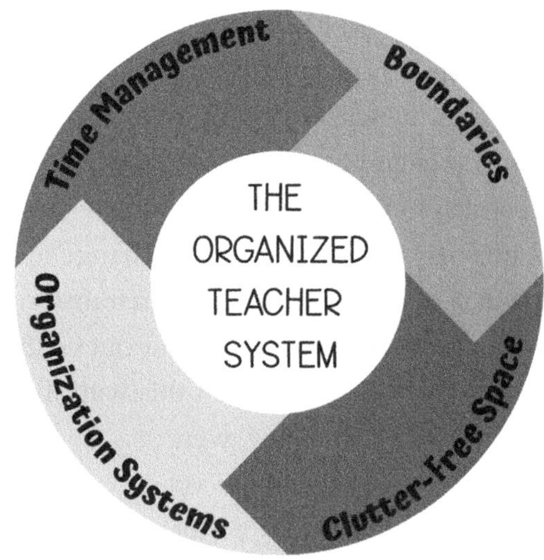

Figure 2.1 Overview of The Organized Teacher System

The Organized Teacher Toolkit

This system isn't about doing more—it's about finally doing what matters in a way that's sustainable. If you want more support and see how these systems will benefit you, I've created The Organized Teacher Club. It's where the full Organized Teacher System lives and includes quick video tutorials, over 100 ready-to-use organization tools (like the ones you'll be getting throughout this book), and a community of supportive teachers who are building these habits right alongside you. It's where you can go when you get stuck and want some extra support.

Let's quickly break down each part of The Organized Teacher System so you can see why it's necessary to implement in your classroom and the impact when you don't (see Figure 2.1).

Boundaries: Protecting Your Time and Energy

The foundation of leaving school on time more often isn't just about working faster or being more efficient, it's about protecting your time like it matters. Because it does. Boundaries aren't about being rigid or inflexible. They're about being clear and intentional with how much of yourself you give to your work each day, and learning to stop before you've emptied the tank completely. They're about making proactive decisions ahead of time so that you don't get swept away by a never-ending to-do list or everyone else's emergencies, and they're the foundation of The Organized Teacher System.

At the most basic level, boundaries are choices. Choices about how late you'll stay. What work (if any) comes home with you. Whether you check your email after school. Whether you say yes to another committee, another student club, another hallway duty, or another "quick favor." These small choices add up. And when you start to make them intentionally, you create structure—not just in your schedule, but in how you show up as a teacher *and* as a person. But let's be honest—it's really easy to forget about your boundaries. It's even easier to ignore them. Especially in education. Teaching is one of the most personal professions out there. You care deeply. You're committed. You want to be the one people can count on. You see a need and your first instinct is to step in and help. And because of that, you probably say yes more than you want to. Not because you don't know better, but because it feels easier in the moment than explaining your no.

How to Leave School Completely Prepared Without Working Nights and Weekends

And it's not just internal pressure—it's cultural. Schools often reward overworking, even if they don't say it out loud. The teacher who stays the latest, volunteers the most, takes on every extra task, and is constantly available tends to be seen as more dedicated, more reliable, more committed. But here's what we don't always talk about: that same teacher is often the one heading toward burnout, stretched too thin, running on fumes. This expectation becomes part of school culture. It becomes *normalized*. As you begin to create boundaries—real ones, not just the kind you talk about, but the kind you actually *follow*—it might feel like you're doing something wrong. It might even feel really uncomfortable. Do it anyway. I started deciding ahead of time what my limits were. I chose a hard stop time for each day. I kept school email off my phone. I stopped responding to messages after hours. I paused before saying yes to anything and gave myself permission to say, "Let me think about it," instead of automatically committing. Was it uncomfortable at first? Absolutely. But the discomfort of setting boundaries is far less than the long-term exhaustion of having none at all.

Here's the thing most people forget: **you can still be a team player and have strong boundaries**. You can be helpful without being available 24/7. You can care deeply about your students and still prioritize your own well-being. And in fact, the more you do, the better you'll show up—for your kids, for your colleagues, and for yourself. Teachers who model boundaries teach students that limits are healthy. That rest is productive. That you don't have to burn out to be good at your job.

Sometimes setting boundaries starts small. Maybe it's deciding you'll only check your email twice a day instead of constantly refreshing it. Maybe it's choosing one day a week where you leave at contract time, no matter what. Maybe it's saying no to a new committee or extra duty, even if you feel a little guilty. Those small shifts add up. And they teach you—slowly but surely—that your time matters just as much as anyone else's.

But I want to be honest here, too: boundaries aren't always easy to maintain. You'll probably set a few and break them. You'll feel pulled back into old habits. You'll get pushback, especially if the people around you are used to you always saying yes. That doesn't mean you're doing it wrong. It means you're doing something *new*. And like any new skill, it takes practice. You're learning how to rewrite your role in a system that thrives on teachers overextending themselves, and that takes immense courage.

The Organized Teacher Toolkit

What helps is having clarity about why you're setting these boundaries in the first place. What do you want more of in your life? Time with your family? Time to rest? Time to actually enjoy your evenings and weekends? Boundaries aren't about saying no just to say no—they're about saying *yes* to something better. Something more aligned with who you want to be both inside and outside the classroom. Those are your core values and something you'll discover more about soon because when you have those, it's easier to actually honor your boundaries.

And once you start, you'll notice a shift. Not just in how you feel, but in how you operate. You'll stop ending each day completely drained. You'll begin to reclaim your energy, your focus, and your time. You'll make fewer reactive decisions and more intentional ones. You'll start teaching in a way that's sustainable—not just for this school year, but for the long haul.

We'll go much deeper into how to set boundaries that actually stick—plus how to handle the guilt, pushback, and tricky situations that come with them—in Chapter 3. For now, just remember this: boundaries aren't walls, and they're not about shutting people out. They're bridges back to the version of you who isn't constantly overwhelmed. They're the foundation for a teaching career that doesn't require you to give up your life. You deserve to teach well *and* live well. Boundaries are how you start doing both, and without boundaries, it's nearly impossible to manage your time well.

Time Management: Making the Most of the Time You Do Have

Time management can feel like one of the most frustrating parts of teaching. You start the day with good intentions—maybe even a plan—and then the bell rings, the emails start, a student has a meltdown, a meeting gets added to your calendar, and suddenly the planning time you were counting on disappears. You're constantly being pulled in a dozen directions, and at the end of the day, you wonder, *What did I even get done?*

If you've ever felt like your time is slipping through your fingers, you're not alone. Most teachers are never taught how to manage their time *as teachers*. You're given endless responsibilities but very little guidance on how to organize them during the school day. There's no manual for how to protect your prep, balance your priorities, or keep

How to Leave School Completely Prepared Without Working Nights and Weekends

from drowning in tasks. Time management in education is different because it has to account for interruptions, unpredictable needs, and constant shifts in expectations. And when the system isn't built to give you enough time, it's easy to blame yourself for falling behind.

That's where This part of The Organized Teacher System comes in. Once you start setting boundaries to protect your time, the next step is learning how to manage that time with intention. And I want to be clear: this doesn't mean packing every second of your schedule with tasks or trying to be "productive" from bell to bell. It's not about doing more—it's about doing what *matters most* with less stress. The goal is not perfection. The goal is clarity and consistency.

Time management isn't just about your schedule. It's about your mental energy, your emotional bandwidth, and your ability to focus. Some teachers feel defeated before the day even starts because their to-do list is overflowing and their brain is already trying to juggle five things at once. Or maybe you're easily distracted and it takes you much longer to complete tasks. That doesn't make you disorganized. That makes you human. But with the right mindset—and later, the right systems—you can shift out of survival mode and start using your time in a way that actually supports you.

I remember one teacher I worked with who told me, "I feel like I'm sprinting through my entire day just trying not to fall behind." She was staying late, working through her lunch, and still couldn't catch up. Once we looked at where her time was actually going, she realized most of her day was being spent reacting—putting out fires, answering last-minute requests, and trying to multitask every second. The shift came when she started to get intentional: protecting a few non-negotiable blocks of time and giving herself permission to stop doing everything at once. It wasn't just about becoming more efficient, it was about taking back control on how she spent her time.

You might be in a season where time feels impossible, where your schedule is full, your energy is low, and your to-do list feels like a monster you can't tame. That's okay. The first step is simply acknowledging that you deserve better. You deserve a workday that doesn't leave you depleted. You deserve to walk out of your classroom feeling accomplished instead of defeated. And that starts by believing that your time matters—not just what you give to your students, but the time you give to yourself.

Part of learning to manage your time well is learning to focus on what matters most in that moment. It's about learning to prioritize, even when everything feels important, and giving yourself permission to let go of the things that can wait. When you can start your day knowing what truly needs your attention—and protect your time long enough to give it your focus—you'll stop spinning your wheels and finally start making real progress. That's what we'll work on in Chapter 4. We'll explore what it actually looks like to manage your time as a teacher in a way that's *realistic and sustainable*. You'll learn how to get clear on your priorities, how to handle those constant distractions (because they're not going away), and how to create a flow to your day that gives you back your evenings and weekends. You'll learn how to move from being reactive to being intentional—so your time doesn't control you, *you* control your time. While I can't magically give you more hours in the day, I can show you a way to use the hours you already have a little better than you're using them right now.

Clutter-Free Space: Why It Matters

Clutter matters more than you think, and according to a UCLA study,[1] it led to increased cortisol levels—your body's main stress hormone—in women. If thinking about your classroom feels suffocating, it's not just the piles and clutter. It's actually everything it represents. It's that constant feeling of never having enough time, so papers pile up, things get shoved into cabinets, and then you're left with this mess. And when you do have a minute to finally go through those stacks, something more demands your attention. All the actual stuff feels heavy but the mental drain of it always weighing on you in the back of your mind takes its toll—the constant feeling of needing to do more, especially as you see the piles growing on your desk and the stuff barely fitting in your cabinets. And every year, you tell yourself you're finally going to get it under control, but there's always more to do and when break finally rolls around, you just want to rest. I know you've got good intentions when you buy all of the organization

---

[1] Saxbe, D.E., and Repetti, R.L. (2010). No place like home: Home tours correlate with daily patterns of mood and cortisol. *Personality and Social Psychology Bulletin*, 36(1), 71–81. UCLA Center on Everyday Lives of Families (CELF).

How to Leave School Completely Prepared Without Working Nights and Weekends

bins and baskets and labels but nothing really changes. You don't need any more organization systems, you need a fresh start first that's actually doable with your busy teacher schedule.

According to the *Journal of Neuroscience*,[2] research in cognitive psychology shows that excess visual stimuli compete for attention and increase cognitive load, making focus and decision-making harder. This can drain teachers' mental energy, especially in visually busy classrooms. And if you're feeling this way, chances are your students are as well.

Let's get your clutter under control and create so you can start with a clean space that you can easily manage throughout the year as you begin to implement organization systems that actually work. The clutter-free part of the system shows you exactly how to clear out what you don't need and organize what you do so you can find things quickly.

Organization Systems: Letting Systems Do the Heavy Lifting

If you're constantly misplacing materials, forgetting what needs to be copied, or redoing tasks you already did last week because you couldn't find them, it's not a reflection of your ability—it's a reflection of not having systems that support you. And without those systems? Every day feels like a scramble. Organization isn't about being naturally tidy or loving labels and color coding (although if that's your thing, great!). It's about building systems that do the thinking for you. Systems reduce decision fatigue. They help you stop wasting time looking for things, redoing work, or figuring it all out on the fly. The most organized teachers aren't more disciplined or better at multitasking—they've simply created routines that support their day-to-day flow.

But here's where most teachers get stuck: they try to get organized in the middle of chaos. You're juggling lesson plans, student needs, communication with caregivers, grading, meetings—and on top of all that, you're supposed to organize your entire

---

[2]McMains, S., and Kastner, S. (2011). Interactions of top–down and bottom–up mechanisms in human visual cortex. *Journal of Neuroscience*, 31(2), 587–597.

classroom while also teaching? No wonder it feels overwhelming. The truth is, you can't create sustainable systems on top of clutter, mental or physical. You have to clear space first. And that can be really hard to do when you move into a classroom where the previous teacher gifted you all of their stuff. Or maybe you just moved grade levels but you've got so much stuff you're holding onto in case you move back to first grade. And that's why so many teachers give up before they even start—they're trying to run a marathon with a backpack full of bricks.

If your classroom feels like it's overflowing with "just in case" supplies, piles of papers you don't know what to do with, old curriculum, or random bins of stuff that no longer serve you, please know: it's not a personal failure. It's the result of a system that expects teachers to hold onto everything, prepare for everything, and do everything—without the proper funding or resources—so you hoard things just in case. You're not behind. You just need a reset. I'll never forget one third-grade teacher I worked with named Melissa. She came into The Organized Teacher Club feeling completely overwhelmed. Her classroom was full of resources she'd collected over the years—bins of centers, stacks of papers, class sets of copies she didn't get to use, piles of anchor charts—but she couldn't find anything when she needed it. She told me, "I have so much good stuff, but it's stressing me out." She was staying late every day just to dig through materials and prep for the next. We didn't start with an elaborate organization plan. We started by clearing one drawer. Then we set up a simple system for her weekly copies. Then we created a routine for student turn-in bins so they weren't all handing her papers at random. Little by little, her classroom transformed—not just physically, but emotionally. She told me later, "I didn't realize how much energy I was spending just *looking* for things." With systems in place, she started leaving on time more often, her students became more independent, and her classroom felt like a place she could finally breathe in again. That's what I want for you. Not perfection. Not an Instagram-worthy classroom. Just systems that work—so you can, too. In Chapters 5 and 6, we'll work on clearing the clutter and setting up a clean space so it finally works for *you*, not against you.

Once the clutter is cleared, that's when organization systems start to stick. This is actually my favorite part. Imagine knowing exactly where your copies are for the week or your students turning in their work without asking where it goes. Imagine not having to reinvent your grading system every quarter or wondering what you said to that parent last month. Systems create structure. Structure saves time. And time gives you

23

peace and freedom. That's the kind of organization we're aiming for—not Pinterest-perfect, but *purposeful. Sounds pretty awesome, right?*

I've worked with thousands of teachers inside The Organized Teacher Club who have felt buried under the weight of disorganization and chaos. They didn't need more hours or more willpower—they needed systems they could easily implement to save time. And when they put those systems in place, everything changed. Their classrooms ran more smoothly, their students were more independent, and most importantly, *they* felt more in control of their day. You don't need to organize every square inch of your classroom overnight. And you definitely don't need to overhaul your entire approach to teaching. What you need is to start small and take baby steps—with one area, one routine, one system—and build from there. In Chapter 11, I'll walk you through the exact areas of your classroom and workflow that benefit the most from strong systems. From managing paperwork and grading to storing student materials and prepping for a sub, we'll break it down so it feels doable, not overwhelming. Because here's the truth: you are already doing the hard part—teaching. Systems aren't about adding more to your plate. They're about making space so you can actually *enjoy* the work you do. When your classroom runs on systems, you free up mental energy, reduce stress, and start showing up as the teacher you truly want to be. And that's exactly what you deserve.

Leaving school prepared and on time isn't a fantasy. It's not reserved for the naturally organized or the teachers with the "easy" grade levels. It's a skill—and like any skill, it can be learned, practiced, and strengthened over time. When you combine boundaries, time management, a clutter-free space, and organization systems, you start teaching *with intention* instead of running on adrenaline and guilt. You start creating a day that works for you—not one that controls you.

What would that make possible for you?

Imagine how your life could feel if your evenings weren't spent catching up on schoolwork. If your weekends were actually restful instead of recovery time. If you walked into Monday morning already feeling caught up.

That's not a pipe dream. That's what happens when you begin to use a system that supports *you,* not just your students. These changes don't require you to overhaul your personality or work 60-hour weeks—they just require small, consistent shifts that build toward something sustainable. And here's what's most important: you are already a great teacher. The goal isn't to prove yourself by doing more. It's to give yourself the space and support you need to keep doing what you love—without burning out. Teaching doesn't have to cost you your peace, your relationships, or your identity outside the classroom. You can leave school prepared *and* have a life. You deserve both.

Task: When you think about teaching, which part of the system are you currently missing?

exxxistence/
Adobe Stock Photo

Chapter 3

Easily Create Boundaries You Can Finally Stick To

Boundaries are essential in any profession, but in teaching, they're non-negotiable if you want to stay in this profession for the long haul. Teaching asks so much of your time, energy, and heart and without clear boundaries, it will take more than you can sustainably give, which is probably why you're reading this book right now! When you don't define what's okay and what's not, the job can quickly bleed into every corner of your life: evenings, weekends, and even your thoughts at 2 a.m. *Boundaries protect your capacity to keep showing up physically, mentally, and emotionally.* They're what keep you from becoming so overwhelmed that you start to lose the very parts of yourself that make you a great teacher in the first place. Boundaries aren't about being difficult or closed off; they're about being clear, and clear is kind. And clarity is one of the most generous things you can offer in a profession built on relationships. There's always another email to answer, another stack of papers to grade, another student who needs you. But if we want to stay in this profession and actually *thrive*, not just survive, we have to stop operating like our time and energy are endless resources. They're not. And that's where boundaries come in and not just as a buzzword, but as an essential tool to protect your peace, preserve your joy, and model healthy behavior for your students. So how do you set boundaries if it's been hard to be consistent with following through?

Your Core Values

Before we can build boundaries that actually feel good and actually stick, you must get clear on *why* those boundaries matter in the first place. Boundaries aren't just about saying no to tasks or people; they're about saying yes to the things that matter most to you. That's where your core values come in. What are core values? They're the non-negotiables in your life that are most important to you *outside* of school. They could be quality time with your own kids, protecting your mental health, being present at home, working out, or doing your favorite hobby. You'll find it's much easier to know where to draw the line at work *when you base your decisions back to your core values, especially when the pressure to overextend yourself creeps in and the things that really matter get put on the back burner again.*

If you've ever felt like you've lost a piece of yourself in teaching, this next exercise is your way back. It's quick, powerful, and has helped thousands of teachers just like you. So think of your core values like your compass. Once you name them, you'll be able to spot the areas where your current habits or boundaries (or lack of boundaries) aren't lining up with what matters most. This isn't about adding more to your plate; it's about bringing clarity to what's already there. And with that clarity, you'll be ready to build boundaries that don't just sound nice, but actually *feel right* in your day-to-day life.

exxxistence/
Adobe Stock Photo

At the end of the day, what are the most important parts of your life outside of teaching? And here's a little hint, they're probably the things that you wish you had more of in your life!

Step 1: Read through the list of core values and circle or highlight any that resonate with you or even add your own. Then narrow it down to 3–5 that feel most aligned with how you want to live and work. They're the things that really light you up and make you smile.

- Family
- Rest
- Creativity
- Connection
- Health

- Honesty
- Joy
- Simplicity
- Growth
- Learning
- Faith or Spirituality
- Adventure
- Kindness
- Financial Stability
- Impact
- Purpose
- Freedom
- Community

Step 2: Get honest with yourself and take a moment to reflect on each of the values you chose and ask:

- How well am I living this value right now?
- Where does this value show up in my daily life?
- Where is it being compromised, especially because of work?

Chances are, you'll most likely see that the things that are most important to you tend to be pushed down on your list in order to fit in everything you need to as a teacher, right? And it's often why you may be feeling defeated or your needs aren't being met. And it's why so many teachers really love the summer and winter break version of themselves because they are making time for the things that really matter to them.

Easily Create Boundaries You Can Finally Stick To

Step 3: For each value, write a sentence that starts with:

- (Value) is important to me because . . .
- I want to honor (value) by . . .
- When I have time for (value), I feel . . .

Now that you're clear on your core values, I want you to keep them close so you can easily refer back to them at school. Save them as your wallpaper on your phone or write them on a Post-it and keep it near your work computer as a visual reminder. They're more than just words, they're your why! Because every time you choose to set a boundary, you're not just saying "no" to something at school, you're saying "yes" to something deeply important in your life. And it's probably what's been missing for you as a teacher.

Creating Boundaries

The next step is to check whether your current boundaries, if you have them, support your core values or quietly compete against them. It's one thing to say that family, rest, or health matters to you, but if you're regularly staying late, bringing work home, or saying yes to things that cut into that time, the value is there in theory but not in practice. That doesn't mean you're doing anything wrong. It just means it's time to realign.

Ask yourself: *Where are my values being honored in my day? Where are they being pushed aside in service of everything else?*

Maybe you value peace, but your schedule feels frantic. Maybe you value connection, but work is consuming your evenings. This is where boundaries become powerful, not as rules, but as a way to *protect* what matters most. Your values aren't just a nice list for your journal and something you make time for when you can. These are the most important parts of your life.

Here's what this looks like in real life. Start by identifying your *non-negotiables*. Maybe it's dinner

The Organized Teacher Toolkit

with your family. Maybe it's your Thursday night yoga class or your standing therapy appointment. Whatever it is, *schedule it first* and treat it like it's as important as IEP meetings or staff PD, because it is. Once it's on your calendar, protect it. Don't squeeze school work around it. Don't say, "just this once." The moment we start making exceptions, we're teaching others, and ourselves, that our time is up for grabs.

Next, set *clear work-hour boundaries*. Choose a time you'll stop working each day and then actually stop. Consider starting small and pick just one day per week that you're leaving on-time, whatever that may be for you. Set a timer or a visual reminder (one teacher I know hangs a sign on her classroom door that says, "Done for the day . . . see you tomorrow!"). Communicate your availability to others. A simple auto-response on your email like: *"I check email between 7:30–4:00. I'll respond within 48 hours during that time frame."* sends a clear message and reduces the pressure to always be "on."

And here's the hard part: *respecting your own boundaries* even when no one else does. That means not grading papers at 10 p.m. just because you're anxious. That means walking away from your desk at your cut-off time, even when your to-do list isn't done. That means letting "good enough" be *enough* on a Thursday when you're exhausted. Boundaries don't just protect your time, they protect your energy, your focus, and your ability to show up as your full self in the classroom.

Real Teacher Talk

Throughout this book, you'll see short "Real Teacher Talk" moments—quick snapshots from teachers who've used the Organized Teacher System in their own classrooms and lives. These aren't long stories or polished case studies. They're honest, real-world reflections from educators who were tired, stretched thin, or overwhelmed . . . and found a better way. My hope is that their voices remind you that you're not alone, and that small, doable shifts can create meaningful change.

I am the only one who can set boundaries for myself, and if I don't respect my boundaries, it will be nearly impossible for me to set boundaries with others. —Melissa W.

Easily Create Boundaries You Can Finally Stick To

Setting Boundaries with Administrators

Let's start with the one that feels the trickiest because I know this is the one that makes most teachers' stomach drop a little. Setting boundaries with administrators can feel uncomfortable, especially if you're worried about how you'll be perceived. But here's the truth: being clear about your capacity doesn't make you difficult, it makes you professional. Clear communication helps prevent burnout, resentment, and misunderstandings. And administrators, especially the good ones, don't want a burnt-out staff.

Setting a boundary might sound like saying no to serving on a committee because you're already leading a grade-level team. It might mean asking to reschedule a last-minute meeting because it overlaps with your only prep time that week. It could look like asking for more clarity before agreeing to a new initiative. These aren't complaints or you being difficult, they're conversations. You can approach them calmly and professionally, rooted in your values. "Thanks for thinking of me. I want to be fully present for what I'm already committed to, so I'll need to pass on this one," is just as valid as a yes.

Remember, boundaries with leadership don't always have to be reactive. You can be proactive, too. If you know certain times of the year stretch you thin, let your administrator know ahead of time what support would help you manage it. You don't need to say yes to everything to be seen as a team player. Showing up with honesty, professionalism, and a clear sense of what you can (and can't) take on, that's what real leadership looks like.

When Things Go Off Track: Five Sentence Frames to Use with Administrators

- "Thank you for thinking of me. I'm currently at capacity with my existing responsibilities and want to give those my full attention."

  (This acknowledges the request while honoring your workload.)

- "I'm happy to support in the future, but right now I need to prioritize my classroom and current commitments."

  (This shows willingness without sacrificing your boundaries in the moment.)

- "I've noticed that staying late is becoming a regular thing, and I'd like to create a better balance so I can show up fully each day. I may need to step back from some of the extra duties I've taken on."

  (This is a gentle way to initiate a conversation about sustainability.)

- "I'm unable to continue being in charge of this committee next semester."

  (This is a way to reduce extra commitments while still being in integrity.)

- "Could we talk about how to streamline this new initiative so it doesn't add extra hours to an already full day?"

  (This opens up dialogue and positions you as a problem-solver, not a complainer.)

Just like setting boundaries with administrators, communicating with colleagues can feel delicate, especially when you're part of a tight-knit team or have built strong friendships at school. You want to be supportive. You want to be collaborative. And chances are, you *are* that person others can always count on. But when "being a team player" starts to mean overextending yourself or picking up the slack for others, it's time to check in with your own needs and capacity. Boundaries with colleagues aren't about pulling away, they're about preserving your energy so you can show up as your best self *and* maintain healthy relationships at work. Let's talk about what that can look like.

Setting Boundaries with Colleagues

It's no secret that your relationships with your colleagues can make or break how your day feels. Some teammates become lifelong friends, and others may unknowingly (or repeatedly) cross lines that drain your time and energy. The challenge? Most oversteps come from a place of good intentions: quick texts to coordinate, spontaneous venting sessions, or "let's just meet during lunch" to get things done. But these habits, over time, chip away at your planning time, your headspace, and your ability to stay on top of your work. Let's talk about some common areas where boundaries with colleagues can quietly slip.

Easily Create Boundaries You Can Finally Stick To

Meeting Norms: If your team meetings always run over or feel disorganized, try suggesting an agenda and end time ahead of time. This was helpful when I was on a team of eight and we had an assigned timekeeper to keep us on task and a notetaker to easily refer back to PLC notes. Figure 3.1 shows an example of PLC notes used to support clear roles and efficient meetings. If you've finished what applies to you, it's okay to politely excuse yourself: "I have to step out to prep for my next block—thanks everyone!"

> *Texting at All Hours:* Just because we *can* text doesn't mean we *should.* Let teammates know you'll only respond to work-related messages during certain hours. You can also turn off notifications without guilt because you're allowed to have uninterrupted time. There's nothing worse than relaxing on the weekend or during break and the team texts about school start rolling in.

> *Respecting Planning Time:* This is big. You don't need to feel bad for using your prep time for what it's intended for: *prepping.* A quick, "Hey, I'm using this time to focus—can we catch up later?" can go a long way. So lock your door, shut your blinds, and even turn off your lights if you must!

> *Sharing the Workload:* Teamwork isn't equal if one person always says yes while others hang back. If your plate is full, speak up. It's okay to say, "I've taken the lead on the last few projects, so I'm going to sit this one out." On my team, we shared the workload and split up planning, making copies, scheduling field trips and special grade-level events, and more. If this isn't something you haven't done yet, it's not too late to suggest it and start.

> *Friendly But Firm Boundaries:* It's possible to be warm *and* clear. If hallway chats are stealing your focus, try: "I'd love to talk more, can we check in after school instead?"

When Things Go Off Track: Five Sentence Frames to Use with Colleagues

- "I totally get the urgency. Can we circle back during our scheduled time so I can stay on track with what I'm working on now?"

  (Use this when you're interrupted during planning or focused work.)

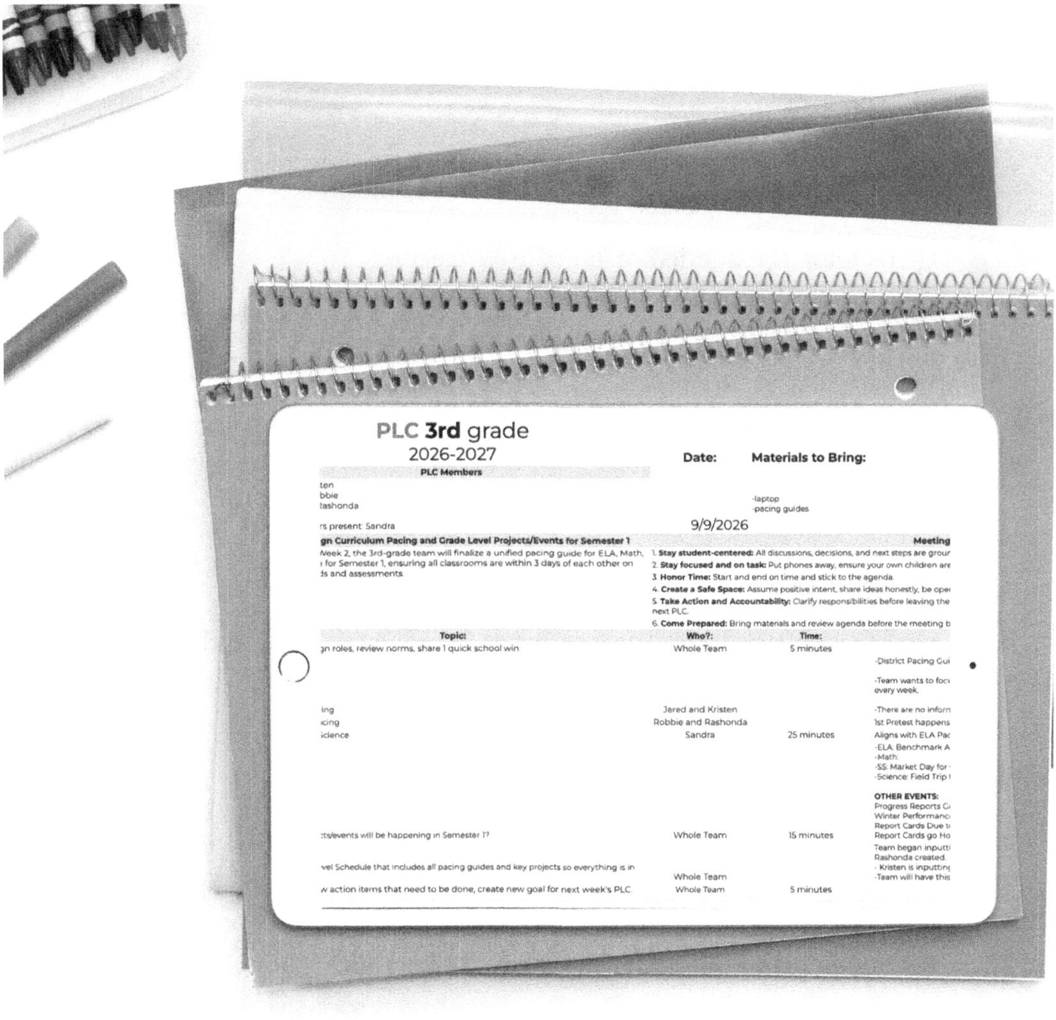

Figure 3.1   PLC notes used to support meeting norms and efficiency

Scan to get this download

Easily Create Boundaries You Can Finally Stick To

- "I've started keeping my evenings free for family/down time, so I may not see messages after school hours. If it's urgent, I'll catch it in the morning."

   (A gentle way to protect your off-hours.)

- "I want to be really present for our meeting, but I need us to stick to the agenda so I can make it to my next block prepared."

   (Helps refocus extended or unfocused meetings.)

- "I've noticed I've taken on a few extras lately. Can someone else take the lead on this one so we keep things balanced?"

   (Encourages shared responsibility without resentment.)

- "I'd love to brainstorm this with you, but I'm in the middle of something right now. Can we schedule a time to talk?"

   (Prevents derailment without dismissing a teammate's needs.)

Just as we set boundaries with our teammates to protect our time and energy, we also need to consider how we engage with families.

Setting Boundaries with Caregivers/Parents

Caregiver communication is such an important part of teaching but it can also become overwhelming if it's not managed intentionally. I remember one year standing in front of a new group of families at Back to School Night telling the adults that they can email me anytime and I'll reply right away. At the time, I thought that was something to be proud of and didn't realize that being so responsive was actually pretty problematic because I accidentally trained parents to expect an almost immediate reply from me.

To avoid my same mistake, let's talk about how to maintain respectful, supportive relationships with caregivers *without* letting communication take over your evenings, weekends, or personal boundaries.

Connecting with families is one of the most important and emotionally charged parts of your job. When it goes well, it creates a team approach that benefits the student.

But when it doesn't, it can leave you feeling disrespected, second-guessed, or emotionally drained. The truth is, no matter how dedicated or communicative you are, there will be moments when a caregiver emails at all hours, questions your professional judgment, or responds in ways that feel combative or even downright rude.

As teachers, you're often conditioned to just "take it," assuming that being available 24/7 or always responding with a smile somehow makes you better at your job. But here's the thing: you can care deeply about your students and still have clear limits around how and when you communicate with families. Boundaries with caregivers aren't about creating distance, they're about creating *structure* so communication can be respectful, manageable, and effective.

> *Rude or Demanding Emails:* You do *not* have to respond immediately or emotionally. Give yourself time to breathe, and remember: you're allowed to keep your responses short, professional, and boundaried. You're the teacher, not the target. Consider waiting 24 hours before responding or even writing out the email you really want to send, but don't. We've got a great tool inside The Organized Teacher Club called "The Organized Teacher Coach" that crafts thoughtful, respectful emails without emotion for you. Perhaps you can have another teacher proofread your email before sending it or ask AI for some help!
>
> *Questioning Your Teaching:* It's normal for caregivers to advocate for their child, but constant questioning or challenging your every move crosses a line. You can redirect these conversations respectfully by reinforcing your decisions and keeping communication student-focused.

When Things Go Off Track: Easy Sentence Frames to Use with Caregivers

Avoid overexplaining or making it personal: Frame your response around the child's needs and the data you're using to guide decisions.

- Example: "Based on the progress I've seen during small-group reading, I'm confident this approach is the best fit right now. I'll continue monitoring and will update you at our next scheduled check-in."

Easily Create Boundaries You Can Finally Stick To

Show proof: Pull in student work, assessment data, or specific examples to help caregivers see that your decisions are based on more than personal opinion.

- Example: "Here's the writing sample from September and one from last week—you can see how his sentence structure and word choice have grown since we started this strategy."

When a caregiver doesn't like your reasoning: If you've already addressed the concern, acknowledge it once more and then move the conversation forward.

- Example: "I hear your concern about the math grouping, and I've explained the reasoning behind it. Let's check in after the next unit to see how your child's confidence and scores are improving."

Disrespect or lack of support: If a caregiver is being inappropriate or dismissive, it's okay to escalate the situation to your admin. You don't have to absorb that on your own.

- Example: "I'd like to keep this conversation productive for [student's name]. Let's continue via email so I can be sure to address your concerns thoroughly."

Emailing at all hours: Just because they send it at 10 p.m. doesn't mean you need to respond at 10:01. Set clear "reply windows" that work for you. Consider setting "office hours" and communicate these hours on your class website and in your email signature so that caregivers know when they can expect to hear from you. Consider taking school email off of your phone and don't check it over the weekend or break so you don't blur the boundaries. After all, I'm sure your school isn't paying for your cellphone bill, right?

- Example: Put an autoresponder on when you leave for the day, weekend, or break that says, "Thanks for reaching out. I'll do my best to respond within 24 hours once I am back at school on (day)."

Wanting to chat in front of students or when a conversation is going overtime: For situations when a parent wants to talk while you're managing your class, helping students, or transitioning to another activity. Keeps the focus on student safety and attention. Here's a few options you can easily use.

- Example: "That's an important topic, and I want to make sure I address it fully. Let's find a time to connect when I'm not responsible for student supervision."

  "I want to be respectful of both your time and mine, can we continue this conversation over email so I can respond thoughtfully?"

  "I'm not able to discuss this right now, but I'm happy to follow up during my office hours or at a scheduled meeting."

  "I appreciate you bringing this to me. Let's set up a time to go over it in detail so we can find a solution together."

Keep these sentence starters in your back pocket to use during tricky moments with the people you get to interact with at school so you can honor your boundaries and stay aligned with your core values you got clear on at the beginning of this chapter.

Should You Take on That Extra Task?

Now that we've talked about why boundaries matter and how to set them, here's where things can get tricky: extra tasks. This is often where even the strongest boundaries get tested. You might have your non-negotiables in place, but then someone pops into your classroom with a "quick" request, or you get an email asking you to join a new committee, and suddenly you're rethinking everything you just committed to.

I'll never forget a teacher in The Organized Teacher Club who swore she had her after-school boundaries down. Then her principal asked if she could "just" help coordinate the school talent show, which was something that sounded small in the moment. Fast forward two months, and she was spending her evenings making flyers, wrangling kids for rehearsals, and fielding parent questions. She ended up staying late three nights a week, not because she wanted to, but because she hadn't paused to consider what that yes would mean for her time, her energy, and her sanity.

Easily Create Boundaries You Can Finally Stick To

It's not always easy to tell in the moment whether you should say yes or no, especially when you care deeply about your school community and want to be helpful. That's why having a clear decision-making process is so important. It gives you a way to pause, reflect, and decide without guilt or pressure, especially if you tend to be a people pleaser.

Before you say yes to anything—whether it's joining a committee, covering a class, or organizing the holiday door-decorating contest—pause and run it through a quick mental checklist. This is where your decision-making flow map comes in and you can easily print it out and keep it near your desk for quick access (see Figure 3.2).

If you can't answer most of these questions with confidence, the flow map leads you to the same place—say no.

Five Ways to Say No

So now you're going to say no, but how? For many teachers, the idea of saying no feels . . . uncomfortable. Teachers are used to being the helpers, the team players, the "yes" people who jump in when something needs to get done. It's part of your identity as an educator and for some of you, part of your identity as people. So when you even

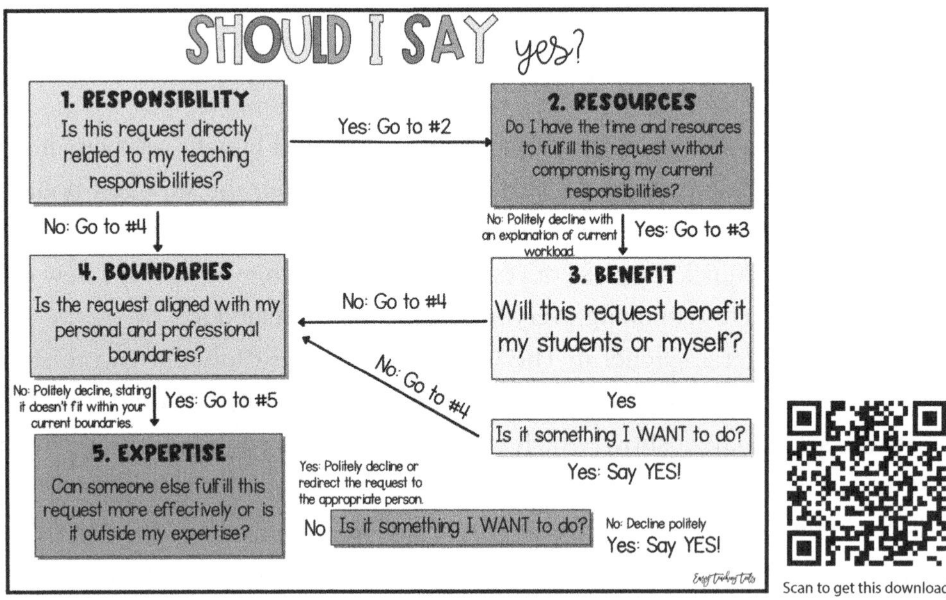

Figure 3.2 Decision-making flow map to help teachers decide to take on extra work

think about saying no, it can feel selfish, aggressive, or like you're letting someone down. Saying no doesn't have to feel confrontational or aggressive, it's about being clear, kind, and firm. It's you deciding what you have the capacity for, what you value, and where your energy will make the most impact. And the discomfort you feel? That's not necessarily a sign you're doing something wrong, it's a sign you're building a new muscle.

It's also worth remembering that, in a school setting, saying yes to too many things has real consequences. Overcommitting can lead to rushed lesson prep, missed grading deadlines, forgotten details, and most importantly, less mental and emotional bandwidth for your students. In other words, protecting your "no" isn't just about you; it's about the quality of your teaching and your well-being over time.

Will people sometimes react poorly when you say no? Yes. Especially if they're used to you always saying yes. But with time, those around you will start to understand your boundaries and respect them. The key is to deliver your "no" with professionalism, kindness, and consistency.

The more you practice, the easier it gets, and the less personal it feels to others. Here are five quick options you can adapt:

1. *The Polite Decline:* "Thanks for thinking of me, but I'm not able to take that on right now."

   Why it works: Warm and appreciative, but still clear. Great for one-off requests from colleagues or parents.

2. *The Values-Based No:* "That's a great project, but it doesn't align with my current priorities."

   Why it works: Shows you're making intentional choices based on what matters most for your students or role.

3. *The Deferred No:* "My plate is full this semester—can you check back with me next term?"

   Why it works: Keeps relationships intact while protecting your current workload.

4. *The Redirect:* "I can't lead this, but maybe [Name] would be a good fit."

   Why it works: Still offers a solution, which softens the refusal.

41

Easily Create Boundaries You Can Finally Stick To

5. *The Firm but Friendly No:* "I'm saying no so I can give my best to the commitments I already have."

Why it works: Confident yet professional; sets a clear boundary without overexplaining.

exxxistence/
Adobe Stock Photo

Task: Pick one of these "no" phrases and practice saying it out loud three times today . . . yes, even if it's just to your mirror or steering wheel. The goal isn't to wait for the perfect moment to use it; it's to get your mouth comfortable forming the words. The more you practice when the stakes are low, the easier it will be to say no calmly and confidently when the stakes are high.

Reading the phrases is one thing and *saying* them out loud is another. In the moment, when a colleague is standing in front of you or an admin is waiting for an answer, it's easy to freeze or slip into an automatic "yes." Practicing in low-pressure situations will help you respond calmly and confidently when it counts. Try these real-life school scenarios and use the "no" options that fit best for you.

Role-Play #1: The Last-Minute Duty Swap
Scenario: It's 2:45 p.m., and a colleague pops in asking if you can cover their dismissal duty *today* because they "forgot" about an appointment.

Practice Saying:

- *Polite Decline:* "Thanks for asking, but I'm not able to take that on right now."

- *Firm but Friendly:* "I'm saying no so I can give my best to the commitments I already have."

Role-Play #2: The "Fun but Extra" Committee
Scenario: Your administrator asks you to join a new after-school committee to plan a school-wide event. You're already stretched thin with grading and family responsibilities.

The Organized Teacher Toolkit

Practice Saying:

- *Values-Based No:* "That's a great project, but it doesn't align with my current priorities."
- *Deferred No:* "My plate is full this semester—can you check back with me next term?"

Role-Play #3: The "Can You Lead This?" Request

Scenario: A colleague emails asking if you can take the lead on a new instructional initiative because "you're so organized."

Practice Saying:

- *Redirect:* "I can't lead this, but maybe [Name] would be a good fit."
- *Polite Decline:* "Thanks for thinking of me, but I'm not able to take that on right now."

Every "no" you say is really a "yes" to something that matters more—your students, your well-being, your family, or your long-term goals. When you connect your response to your values, it stops feeling like rejection and starts feeling like alignment.

exxxistence/
Adobe Stock Photo

Task: Now that you've got a little practice, let's reflect!

1. Which "no" felt the most natural for you to say?
2. Which one felt the most awkward—and why?
3. How did it feel in your body to say it out loud? (Tense shoulders? Relaxed? Nervous laugh?)
4. In what upcoming situation might you realistically need to use it?

The goal isn't to force yourself into a single "perfect" response but to notice which approaches align best with your communication style and values so you can reach for them with confidence when the moment comes.

10 Boundaries to Implement Right Now

Now that you have strategies for saying no with confidence, it's time to put that skill into action with 10 practical boundaries you can start using right away. If you wait until you're completely burned out to set boundaries, it's already too late. These 10 simple shifts will help you protect your time, lower your stress, and stay energized for the parts of teaching you actually love. Implementing even one of them now can make an immediate difference in how you feel at the end of each day.

1. Set a hard stop time each day and stick to it.

2. Keep school email off your phone (or at least notifications off).

3. Only check and respond to email at two designated times per day.

4. Close your classroom door during planning to signal you're not available for interruptions.

5. Avoid eating lunch at your desk daily, use it as a break.

6. Create a standard response for non-urgent requests from colleagues or caregivers.

7. Protect one afternoon or morning a week for uninterrupted work time.

8. Store your grading at school, don't bring it home unless it's truly urgent.

9. Set expectations for student and caregiver communication response times (e.g., 24 hours).

10. Limit how many extra committees, events, or responsibilities you take on per semester.

Boundaries aren't about doing less for your students. They're about doing your best for them without losing yourself in the process. Every time you protect your time, say no to something that doesn't serve you, or choose rest over more work, you're building a sustainable career and a healthier life. You don't have to be the first car in the parking lot or the last one out to prove you're a good teacher. The truth is, the teachers who last in the teaching profession and who truly thrive are the ones who protect their energy, focus on what matters most, and leave school with enough of themselves left to enjoy life outside the classroom.

Setting boundaries isn't a onetime event; it's an ongoing practice. Some days you'll hold them with ease; other days, you might slip and say yes when you meant no. You'll take work home "just this once," or skip your lunch break to catch up. That doesn't mean you've failed; it means you're human, and you're learning.

The key is to notice when you've drifted, give yourself grace, and course-correct before those old habits take over again. Every boundary you set is a promise to yourself and you are worth keeping that promise. Your best teaching doesn't come from running yourself into the ground; it comes from showing up rested, focused, and fully present. So when you catch yourself sliding back into overcommitment, pause, take a breath, and realign with what matters most. Your students and family need you at your best and so do you.

Real Teacher Talk

Before we move on, I want you to hear from a real teacher who's used The Organized Teacher System to make meaningful change. These "Real Teacher Talk" stories come straight from the classroom and are honest, unfiltered reflections from educators who decided to set boundaries, get organized, and take back their time. My hope is that as you read their story, you'll see what's possible for you, too.

I have more time to hang with my toddlers without feeling guilty and distracted. —Allison T.

My family loves having mom back! I have been able to take my children to their activities after school, I go to yoga once a week, I have been able to start reading again (for fun!), and I have been more involved with my third child than I feel like I was for the first two. It feels wonderful to know I have energy after school to play with my kids instead of being mentally and physically drained at the end of the school day. —Sabrena B.

I have SO much more time to devote to friends and family, and I was even able to take on a new volunteer opportunity, which fills me with such joy. —Lisa S.

I now have a personal life! I've taken up going to the gym so I can be healthy and happy. —Monica S.

Easily Create Boundaries You Can Finally Stick To

As we move into building actual boundaries, these values will guide you. They'll help you filter your decisions, big and small. When someone asks you to stay late, take something on, or respond outside of hours, you'll have something solid to come back to: *Does this align with my values? Or does it pull me away from them?* Boundaries aren't just about protecting your time. They're about protecting your ability to live in alignment with who you are and how you want to feel at school *and* at home and that's pretty powerful!

Now that you've seen how boundaries work and what's possible for other teachers who put them in place, it's your turn!

exxxistence/
Adobe Stock Photo

Task: Write out one boundary related to your most important core value and be specific. Don't forget to put it on a Post-it note next to your computer or set an alarm or reminder on your phone to ensure you follow it!

The Organized Teacher Toolkit

Chapter 4

Time Management: Work Smarter, Not Harder

If boundaries are the guardrails that keep your workday from running off course, time management is the roadmap that helps you get where you need to go without taking the long, stressful route that you may be experiencing right now. And here's the truth: once your boundaries are in place, it becomes much easier to manage your time. Why? Because you've already decided when you're leaving school, what's coming home with you (if anything), and what's not. That means the time you *do* have is more precious and you'll naturally be more intentional and want to use it wisely.

Time management for teachers isn't about cramming every second of your day with tasks or creating a Pinterest-perfect schedule. It's about being intentional with your limited time so you can focus on what truly matters and leave the building knowing you're prepared for tomorrow. That means prioritizing tasks that have the biggest impact on your teaching, streamlining repetitive work, and learning to let go of the things that simply aren't worth the energy. In this chapter, we'll talk about how to value your time, teach others to respect it, and use simple, realistic techniques to make your planning and grading more efficient so you can work smarter, not longer.

Here's the thing: it's nearly impossible to manage your time effectively when you haven't set boundaries. Think about it, if you've committed to leaving school at 4:00, you'll naturally become more focused during your prep periods. You're less likely to waste time chatting in the copy room or wandering aimlessly around your classroom because you know your time is limited. But if your end time is flexible, or worse, "whenever I get everything done," you'll fill every available minute, which usually means staying late.

Boundaries create urgency, and urgency creates focus. When you know exactly how much time you have, you start asking better questions: *What's the most important thing I can finish in this block? What can I push to tomorrow? What can I delegate or simplify?* Without those guardrails, it's all too easy to drift from one small task to another—answering a quick email, rearranging a shelf, updating a bulletin board—while the truly important work waits until the end of the day, forcing you to stay late or bring it home. That's what Sabrena did before using The Organized Teacher System and I bet you can relate to her story below.

Does this sound like you? If it does, you're not alone.

Real Teacher Talk

"I always thought I could stay 'just a little longer' and it would help me feel better in the morning when I would get back to my classroom. I would be the first one in the parking lot, and the last one to leave. The thing I hated the most was being the first person to drop my children off at daycare in the mornings, and the last one to pick them up. I missed SO much time with my own kids because I thought I had to do it all at school. I had no boundaries, I didn't know how to say no, I didn't know when I had reached my limit of what I could handle." —Sabrena B.

Valuing Your Time and Teaching Others to Respect It

The truth is, teachers are conditioned to treat their time like it's free and endlessly available. We skip lunch to finish grading, stay after school for "just one more" thing, or take on extra duties without considering the personal cost. But your time is every bit as valuable as your administrator's, your colleagues', or anyone else's in the building. And because so much of your job requires mental focus, creativity, and emotional energy, your time is arguably your most important resource.

Valuing your time means recognizing that every "yes" comes at a cost. Saying yes to covering a class during your prep period means saying no to getting ahead on tomorrow's lessons. Saying yes to another committee means saying no to having free evenings at home. The more you begin to see your time as a nonrenewable resource, something to be budgeted and protected, the more confident you'll feel about using it wisely.

One mindset shift that helps is to treat your prep periods and before/after school time like scheduled appointments with yourself. If a colleague asks you to be a grade-level lead, which means extra meetings and more responsibility, you can politely decline. You can and should protect your own time in the same way. It's not selfish; it's professional.

Here's the truth that may be uncomfortable to admit: people will treat your time the way you allow them to. If you consistently answer emails at night, caregivers will expect you to be available 24/7. If you drop everything to help a colleague in the middle of your prep, they'll learn that you're someone who can be interrupted. It's not that people are trying to take advantage of you, they simply respond to the patterns you set.

And here's the hard part: for many of us, those patterns were set without us even realizing it. Maybe you were the "new teacher" eager to make a good impression, so you said yes to every request. Or maybe you've always been the reliable one in your grade level team, so you became the go-to person when something needed to get done quickly. Over time, these habits become your unspoken job description. The problem is, they also eat away at your time, energy, and focus.

Teaching people to respect your time isn't about becoming unhelpful or shutting your door to everyone, it's about modeling healthy professional boundaries so that your role (and your day) is sustainable. The first step is clarity. You need to know and communicate when you're available and when you're not. That might look like telling colleagues, "I'm in focused planning time right now, but I can help you after lunch," or letting caregivers know in your welcome letter that you respond to emails within 24 hours on school days.

Consistency truly is your secret weapon here. If you answer one email at 8 p.m. but ignore another sent at the same time, you send mixed messages. People will assume "sometimes she's available after hours" instead of "she responds during the school day." The same goes for interruptions; especially if you usually stop everything when someone walks in, the message is "My time is flexible," not "I'm in the middle of something important."

It can feel awkward at first, especially if you've been a "yes" person for a long time. There might be guilt. There might be pushback. But over time, you'll find that when you protect your own time, others will adjust, and in many cases, they'll

Time Management: Work Smarter, Not Harder

respect you more for it. You'll also be setting a quiet example for newer teachers who may not yet realize it's okay to do the same. And here's something to keep in mind: people often go to the person who will say yes. If you've built a reputation for being that person, breaking the pattern won't just free up your time, it might encourage others to step in and share the load.

When you start protecting your time with intention, you're not just preserving your own sanity but you're also training the people around you to interact with you in a way that works for everyone. That's when your time stops feeling like it's constantly being taken from you and starts becoming something you actually control, which is pretty powerful.

Techniques for Prioritizing Tasks and Managing Time Effectively

Once you've put boundaries in place and taught people how to respect them, the next step is making sure the time you *do* have is used wisely. The reality is, not everything on your to-do list carries the same weight. Some tasks are mission-critical, others are nice to get done if you have the time, and some, let's be honest, don't really matter in the big picture at all. *The challenge for teachers is that everything feels important in the moment,* especially when you have students, parents, administrators, and colleagues all needing something from you.

But here's the thing: if everything is a priority, then nothing is.

The most effective teachers I've worked with have one thing in common: they're ruthless about deciding what matters most each day and letting the rest wait. That doesn't mean they're neglecting responsibilities; it means they're intentional about sequencing their work so the most impactful tasks get done first.

One strategy that can help is thinking about your work in three categories:

1. *Must Do*—Non-negotiable tasks that need to be completed today (like prepping materials for tomorrow's lesson or finalizing progress report comments).

2. *Should Do*—Important tasks that need attention soon, but could wait a day or two if needed (like drafting next week's newsletter or reorganizing a supply bin).

3. *Nice to Do*—Tasks that would be great to accomplish if you have extra time but won't cause any harm if they're delayed (like updating a bulletin board or creating new decor for the reading corner).

The trap many teachers fall into is spending too much time in the "Nice to Do" category because those tasks feel satisfying and low-pressure. For example, color-coding your math manipulatives might give you a dopamine boost, but if it means you're staying late to finish lesson plans, it's not the best use of your time.

And then there's the *distraction spiral*, you know the one where the moment you sit down to tackle something important, you get pulled into a chain reaction of unrelated tasks. Maybe you go to grab a pen and notice the date hasn't been changed on the whiteboard, so you fix that. On the way back, you see uncharged Chromebooks, so you plug them in. Then you notice paper scraps on the floor from art time, so you clean them up. Just as you're about to sit down again, your email dings. You check it "just in case" it's important, but instead, it's a message from the one person you really didn't want to hear from right now. Suddenly, you're scrolling social media to avoid thinking about it, and before you know it, 15 minutes are gone.

If that story feels familiar, you're not alone. There's actually research that explains why this happens, and why it's so easy to waste time without realizing it. It's called Parkinson's Law,[1] and it says that *work expands to fill the time available for its completion* (see Figure 4.1). In other words, if you give yourself three hours to create lesson plans, it will take three hours. But if you give yourself 45 minutes, you'll probably finish in 45 minutes. The task itself hasn't changed, only the container of time you've given it. By shrinking your available time, you create urgency and focus, which naturally cuts out unnecessary steps, perfectionistic tinkering, or distractions that stretch the task out longer than it needs to be.

Once you know your true priorities, you can use this principle to your advantage. One of my favorite tools for doing exactly this is the Time Timer Method. I'm going to show you several proven systems from the Organized Teacher System to help you stay focused and manage your time better so you can leave school while it's still light out without bringing work home. Once you know your priorities, you can use these systems to help you stay focused, which is pretty empowering.

---

[1] Parkinson, C. N. (1958). *Parkinson's Law: Or, the Pursuit of Progress.* John Murray.

51

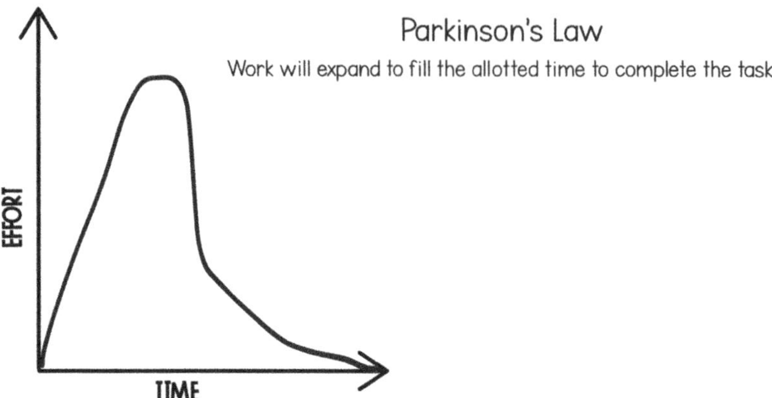

Figure 4.1   Illustration of Parkinson's Law as it relates to teacher time management

The Time Timer Method

Once you've set your boundary, like leaving at 4:00 to get to the gym, and you are familiar with Parkinson's Law, you get to be more intentional with your time. My favorite tool is the Time Timer because it's a visual timer that will remind you how much time you have left so you're not wasting time (see Figure 4.2). What I love about it is that it will beep when the time is up. I used it throughout the day with

Figure 4.2   The Time Timer is a visual reminder tool to help you manage your time

The Organized Teacher Toolkit

my students to help them manage their time but also used it with myself. It's the very best way to hold yourself accountable. If you know you only have 45 minutes to plan, set your timer and do nothing else but plan. No email. No chatting in the hallway. No "just real quick" laminating. The goal is to train your brain to stay locked in until the timer runs out. To help you avoid distractions, try this:

- Lock your door.

- Shut the blinds.

- Put your phone on airplane mode or across the room.

- Respect the timer (more on this in a moment).

But let me ask you this, and I probably already know what you are going to say.

You're most likely going to either ignore it and keep working, reset it, or maybe you'll leave and make it to your gym appointment that you committed to. The majority of the thousands of teachers I've worked with typically continue working because their to-do list is just never ending, right? And the

What do you do when the timer goes off and you're not done?

next thing you know, it's dark outside, your spouse is texting you again wondering where you're at, and you're grabbing that stack of grading and finally heading home.

So here's what you get to try going forward and it may be brand new for you but I encourage you to *respect the timer*. That means when it goes off, stop that task, even if you're not done. If you're feeling panicked just thinking about stopping, it's okay. I know, that's painful to hear, and if you're a perfectionist or a chronic overworker, your instinct will be to keep going. But this is where the magic happens. Respecting the timer forces you to honor the boundaries you've set for yourself. It also teaches you to identify what *actually* needs to get done now and what can wait until tomorrow. The more you practice, the more you'll notice your productivity skyrocket, because you're no longer working with an endless runway of time and instead you've got a focused, finite window, and you'll instinctively make better use of it. Over time, you'll see Parkinson's Law in action. You'll realize that the lesson plan you used to spend two

53

Time Management: Work Smarter, Not Harder

hours perfecting can actually be done in 40 minutes without sacrificing quality. And you'll get that irreplaceable feeling of walking out the school doors on time, with work done, and the rest of your day ahead of you—something you might not have thought possible before.

Put a Note on Your Door

If self-control is an area you could improve upon and you want to talk to everyone who comes into your room, put a note on your door letting people know that you are planning and to come back another time (see Figure 4.3)! If you're worried what people will think, it's not your worry to take on! Do what you need to preserve your planning and prep time. I encourage teachers in The Organized Teacher Club to laminate this note and use a magnet to keep it on the inside of your door so you can easily place it outside when you need it.

Figure 4.3   Put a note on your door

Chrome Extensions to Increase Productivity

If you're like most teachers, lesson planning today happens at least partly on your computer, whether you're searching for resources, tweaking slides, updating your Learning Management System (LMS), or answering parent emails. The problem? Your computer is also home to your biggest distractions. One "quick" peek at your email can turn into a half-hour detour. You hop on Pinterest for a math center idea and suddenly you're pinning pumpkin recipes. It's not that you don't have self-control (or may be it is), it's that the internet is designed to grab your attention and keep it.

This is where free Chrome extensions can be game-changing. Think of them as guardrails for your focus during planning time. Pick just one to try out to help you increase your productivity.

Mindful Browsing—Instead of flat-out blocking websites, Mindful Browsing gives you a gentle nudge when you head toward a distracting site. It asks you to pause and decide if you really want to visit that page. That moment of mindfulness can be enough to redirect you back to the lesson plan you were working on.

Stay Focused—This one is perfect if you know you only need *five minutes* to check a site but don't want to get sucked in. StayFocusd lets you set daily time limits for distracting websites, so once your time is up, those sites are blocked for the rest of the day.

Pause—Simple but powerful, Pause forces you to literally wait for a few seconds before a site loads. That short delay can give your brain the space to ask, "Do I really need to go there right now?" You'd be surprised how often the answer is "No," and you just click away.

Pro Tip: Install only one extension at a time, so you can get used to it and see how it fits into your routine. Once it becomes second nature, add another. Think of these tools like classroom routines; they work best when they're consistent and intentional.

Time Management: Work Smarter, Not Harder

Task: Pick one Chrome extension to install on your school and work computer right now.

exxxistence/
Adobe Stock Photo

Real Teacher Talk

One of our Organized Teacher Club members, Megan, used to lose at least 30 minutes of her prep period every day without even realizing it. She'd open her laptop to write math plans, but a quick "just checking email" would turn into responding to five caregiver questions, browsing for bulletin board ideas, and glancing at Instagram "just for a minute." After installing Mindful Browsing and Stay Focused, she started catching herself *before* she got pulled in. Mindful Browsing would pop up when she clicked on social media and remind her of her actual goal. Stay Focused cut her email scrolling down to 10 minutes a day. Within two weeks, Megan was finishing her math plans before the bell and leaving school with time to go to the gym.

Done Is Better Than Perfect Theory

If you've been teaching for more than five minutes, you've probably discovered that your to-do list has no end. Once you get close to completing it, more gets added. Lesson plans, grading, data entry, parent emails, bulletin boards, meetings, professional development . . . the list goes on. And that's just the official list. There's also the mental list: reminding yourself to pick up more Expo markers, helping a student find their missing sweatshirt, reorganizing your classroom library for the third time this year, and baking cupcakes for the Friday fundraiser because you said yes before thinking it through. Somewhere in all that hustle, teachers often get stuck chasing an impossible standard: perfection. We tweak our lesson slides for the fifth time before bed. We stay after school "just a little longer" to make our bulletin board Pinterest-worthy. We spend hours crafting the perfect parent email. And while our intentions are good, that perfectionism comes at a cost: less time for ourselves, less energy for our students, and more burnout. This is where the Done Is Better Than Perfect mindset comes in.

"Done Is Better Than Perfect" doesn't mean lowering your standards or not caring about your work. It means recognizing that the value of a completed task, especially one done well enough to meet its purpose, far outweighs the value of an endlessly polished, incomplete project. It's about understanding that the goal isn't perfection, it's progress. It's about delivering something that works, moves the needle forward, and gets checked off your list so you can move on to the next thing. For teachers, this mindset is powerful because our jobs are never "finished" in the traditional sense. There's always another lesson to prepare, another student to help, another area to improve. If we wait until something is "perfect," we'll be waiting forever. And if we're being honest, your students aren't going to care one way or the other, and at the end of the day, the goal is to ensure they're learning, right?

Perfectionism feels productive, but it's actually a time thief in disguise. Here's how it shows up for teachers:

- *Overpreparing:* Spending hours on a single lesson plan because you want it to be flawless, even if a good plan would serve your students just as well. I'm talking about classroom transformations, elaborate lessons you've always done but maybe this year you just don't have capacity for it, and anything that takes a ton of time (especially if it's because you want it to look good for social media). At the end of the day, ask yourself, "Who is this really for?"

- *Overediting:* Rewriting the same email multiple times instead of sending it when the first draft was already clear and professional. No need to continue to overthink to have it be "just right." Just send it and move on!

- *Overcomplicating:* Adding unnecessary elements to projects (like intricate bulletin boards or overly complex assignments) that don't *significantly* improve student learning. Does that mean you can't ever do them? Absolutely not! But you only have so many hours in the day, so consider spreading out more detailed lessons or bigger projects.

Time Management: Work Smarter, Not Harder

- *Avoiding Completion:* Waiting to start or finish a task because you're afraid it won't be perfect, which creates unnecessary stress and missed deadlines. When you let go of the need for perfection, you create space for efficiency. You finish more tasks in less time, which frees you up for higher-priority work and for your own life outside school. I can assure you that your students don't care if your bulletin board borders are perfectly even!

If perfectionism is something you can relate to, how does it show up in teaching for you?

Consider prioritizing tasks by impact. Instead of spending equal time on everything, you identify which tasks will make the biggest difference for your students and focus your energy there. Then set time limits and give yourself a reasonable amount of time to complete a task and respect the timer and stop when the time is up, trusting that "good enough" is enough which will reduce decision fatigue. It will also save you time and help you avoid getting stuck in an endless loop of "Should I change this?" and "What if I . . ." because you've decided to be satisfied with a functional, complete product. This is one way to prevent burnout and protect your energy by refusing to pour extra hours into things that don't truly need them.

Applying the "Done Is Better Than Perfect" mindset into your teaching life:

80/20 Rule: To make this more actionable, consider adopting the 80/20 rule. The 80/20 rule (also called the Pareto Principle) says that 80% of your results come from 20% of your efforts. For teaching, that means most of your student growth comes from a small set of high-impact actions, things like clear instruction, timely feedback, and building relationships. Ask yourself: *Will spending another 30 minutes tweaking this really improve student learning, or is it just for my own satisfaction?* If it's the latter, stop and move on.

Set Hard Limits: You can also set hard limits for your prep and grading. If you give yourself unlimited time, a task will take unlimited time. Instead, set your Time Timer for 45 minutes for lesson planning, 30 minutes for grading, etc. When the timer goes off, wrap it up. This forces you to make decisions more quickly and helps you finish without overthinking.

Use Templates and Routines: Instead of reinventing the wheel, create or borrow templates for parent emails, lesson plans, or classroom procedures. A good template gets you 80% of the way there instantly. Then you just add the finishing touches. Teachers inside The Organized Teacher Club have a library of templates to choose from when writing report card comments, creating centers, classroom slides, and more to save time!

Batch Similar Tasks: If you're printing, copy all your materials for the week in one trip. Find the time of the day when the copy machine is typically free and get it all done so you aren't cramming during recess. If you're grading, grade all of one assignment type in one sitting. Batching reduces start-stop time and helps you finish big chunks of work without getting bogged down. In Chapter 9, I'll share how to create copy clips to make copying even faster!

Decide What's "Good Enough" in Advance: This one's really important! Before starting, define what "done" looks like because if you don't, you'll continue working way longer than you should. If you're lesson planning, ensure it's aligned to standards, has clear objectives and the student materials ready. When replying to caregivers or writing a class newsletter, use a professional tone, include all key info, spell check, and that's it! It doesn't have to be perfect! When you're working on a bulletin board, set a timer and then ensure student work is displayed neatly and then stop. You don't need three borders that are changed out every month or updated lettering. Keep it simple!

Time Management: Work Smarter, Not Harder

Let Students Take Ownership: If a bulletin board takes you two hours, but students could help assemble it in 20 minutes, let them. It won't look as perfect as if you did it, but it will be done and they'll take pride in their work. I'll share more about the very best bulletin board that doubles as a student memory book that goes home at the end of the year later in the book.

Practice Saying "This Is Enough": When you feel the urge to add "just one more thing," pause and ask yourself:

- *Is this extra step worth my time?*
- *Will it make a measurable difference for my students?*
- *Do I want to do this? Or is it just perfectionism talking?*

If you say no to any of these, skip it!

Real Teacher Talk

Instead of writing paragraphs of feedback on every student essay, I use a pre-made comment bank. I spend five minutes per paper instead of fifteen, which means papers go back in three days instead of two weeks. —Yolanda S.

Many teachers feel like "done is better than perfect" means they're letting their students down. But remember: your students don't need you to be perfect, they need you to be present, energized, and consistent. A perfectly color-coded Google Slide isn't going to make the same difference in a child's learning as a rested teacher who has time to connect with them one-on-one.

The truth is, you can do anything—but you can't do everything. And if you try to do everything perfectly, you end up sacrificing your time, health, and joy.

Next time you're deep in the weeds of a task, repeat this to yourself: *"It's not about being perfect. It's about progress."* The faster you get something done (while meeting its purpose), the more time you free up for other important work or for rest, which is equally important. Perfectionism is a sneaky thief of teacher time. It disguises itself as dedication, but it's really just a form of procrastination that leads to overwhelm and burnout. By embracing the Done Is Better Than Perfect mindset, you reclaim hours of your week, reduce stress, and make space for what matters most, both inside and outside the classroom. You'll never get to the bottom of your to-do list, but you can get to the bottom of your *must-do* list. And that's the difference between a teacher who's just surviving and one who's truly thriving. So, give yourself permission to stop tweaking and start finishing. Your work and your life will be better for it.

The Let It Go Method: Protecting Your Time, Energy, and Sanity

Once you start finishing tasks without overpolishing them, the next step is learning to release the ones that don't truly need your time or attention in the first place, which is where the Let It Go Method comes in. The Let It Go Method is about identifying what's essential, releasing the rest, and freeing up your time and energy for what truly matters both in your classroom and in your life.

Letting go doesn't mean lowering your standards or caring less. It means making intentional choices about where to invest your attention. If something doesn't move you toward your teaching goals, support your students' growth, or protect your well-being, it's a candidate for letting go.

Think of it like cleaning out your mental and physical "teacher bag." When it's stuffed with things you don't need, you can't find the things you do need quickly and you end up lugging around unnecessary weight.

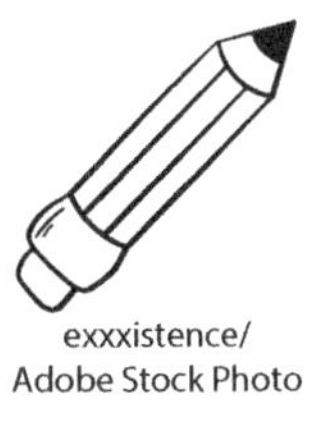

Task: What three classroom tasks can you apply to the "Done is Better Than Perfect" mindset?

exxxistence/
Adobe Stock Photo

Why Teachers Struggle to Let Go

Teachers hang on because:

- They think they *might* need it someday.

- They feel responsible for everything and everyone.

- They're emotionally invested in "how it's always been done."

- They equate busyness with dedication.

- They think it's what makes them a good teacher.

But holding on to everything leads to visual and mental clutter, overwhelmed schedules, and mental exhaustion. The cost is too high.

Apply the Let It Go Method

Consider dropping the "shoulds" and choose intentional action instead. One of the heaviest loads teachers carry isn't in their lesson plan book or their inbox, it's in the invisible list of "shoulds" running through their heads all day. How many times have you ever said, *I should make this lesson more creative. I should decorate for the holidays. I should take on that extra duty. I should answer emails right away. I should be leaving at contract time more often.*

These "shoulds" often come from habit, comparison, or unspoken pressure from others, not from what your students truly need or what matters most to you. Over time, they create overcommitment, overwhelm, and the constant sense that whatever you're doing, it's not enough. The problem with "should" is that it's rooted in obligation, not choice. It makes you feel like you're reacting to demands instead of acting with purpose. Replace "I should" with "I get to." This small change helps you focus on what's meaningful, not just what's expected.

- *I should stay late to finish this bulletin board* → I get to leave on time so I have the energy to be present with my students tomorrow.

- *I should redo this lesson slide to match my theme* → I get to keep it as-is and use the extra time to give meaningful feedback on student work.

- *I should join that committee* → I get to say no so I can focus my energy on improving small group instruction this year.

When you reframe your thinking with "I get to," you're reminded that you have agency. You're making decisions that align with your values, protect your time, and ultimately help you show up as the best version of yourself for your students and for you. Use the following chart to help you reframe. Below are common "should" thoughts teachers have and how to turn them into empowering "I get to" statements that align with your priorities and protect your well-being.

Teacher "I Should" → "I Get To" Conversion Chart

Planning and Prep

Common Teacher "Should"	Empowered "I Get To" Reframe	Why It Works
I should retype these lesson plans to look neater.	I get to use the extra time to prepare hands-on activities my students will love.	Focuses on student engagement over appearance.
I should plan something new for every unit.	I get to reuse and improve strong lessons that worked well last year.	Saves time while still enhancing quality.
I should rewrite all my lesson objectives so they sound fancier.	I get to keep my objectives clear and use that time to gather student feedback.	Puts clarity and student voice over presentation.
I should create custom worksheets for each student.	I get to adapt existing resources so my students' needs are met without starting from scratch.	Maximizes efficiency without sacrificing differentiation.

Time Management: Work Smarter, Not Harder

Grading and Feedback

Common Teacher "Should"	Empowered "I Get To" Reframe	Why It Works
I should take stacks of grading home every weekend.	I get to set a grading limit so I can recharge and return Monday ready to teach.	Encourages boundaries to prevent burnout.
I should fix every student's work so it's perfect.	I get to let students learn from their mistakes so they build resilience.	Focuses on student growth over perfectionism.

Communication and Collaboration

Common Teacher "Should"	Empowered "I Get To" Reframe	Why It Works
I should answer every email as soon as it comes in.	I get to check emails at my scheduled times so I can stay focused on teaching.	Protects deep work time and reduces distraction.
I should respond to every parent concern in detail right away.	I get to give thoughtful responses during my scheduled communication time.	Ensures communication is professional and not rushed.
I should spend my prep time chatting with colleagues so I'm not rude.	I get to use my prep for uninterrupted work so I feel less stressed later.	Protects valuable planning time without guilt.
I should attend every optional training offered.	I get to choose PD sessions that directly support my teaching goals.	Ensures learning is relevant and impactful.
I should agree to cover classes whenever asked.	I get to say yes when I can and no when I need to protect my schedule.	Encourages selective generosity without burnout.

64

Classroom Environment

Common Teacher "Should"	Empowered "I Get To" Reframe	Why It Works
I should decorate my classroom for every holiday.	I get to keep my space simple so it's easier to maintain and less stressful to reset.	Reduces time and money spent on low-impact tasks.
I should make this lesson match the latest Pinterest trend.	I get to keep what's already working so I can spend time on what needs improvement.	Prioritizes results over trends.
I should laminate every single resource so it lasts forever.	I get to decide which items are worth the effort and let the rest go.	Balances durability with realistic time investment.
I should fix that messy bulletin board right now.	I get to schedule it for next week when I have more bandwidth.	Prevents reactive time drains by planning intentionally.

Boundaries and Well-Being

Common Teacher "Should"	Empowered "I Get To" Reframe	Why It Works
I should volunteer for that committee.	I get to protect my planning time so I can improve my small group instruction.	Aligns commitments with instructional goals.
I should buy all the supplies myself to make things easier.	I get to request donations or use what's available so I'm not overspending.	Protects personal finances and sets healthy boundaries.

Time Management: Work Smarter, Not Harder

| I should check in on every single student every day. | I get to rotate my attention so all students get meaningful interactions over time. | Makes connection sustainable and intentional. |
| I should stay late to finish my bulletin board. | I get to leave on time so I have the energy to connect with my students tomorrow. | Shifts priority from aesthetics to meaningful presence. |

Release What You Can't Control

After reframing how you think about what you should be doing, consider releasing what you can't control, and there's a lot as a teacher, right? Dwelling on district policies, administrative decisions, high-conflict coworkers or caregivers, or unpredictable events drains energy you could be using for things within your control. Try a few of these ideas to help you manage the emotions that come with teaching.

- *Sort Into Buckets:* Can I control this, influence it, or neither? Focus only on the first two.

- *Have a Mental Offload Ritual:* End the day by jotting down frustrations, then leave them on paper.

- *Keep Backup Plans:* For schedule changes, have ready-to-go filler activities so you can pivot without stress. One great way to do this is to keep all of your unused class sets of copies that you didn't get to in one place and then grab them when you need them!

- *Practice Reframing:* When you hit an obstacle, shift from "This ruins everything" to "Here's how I'll adapt."

Step-by-Step Plan to Start Letting Go

Once you've identified the things you can't change and given yourself permission to set them down, the next step is to turn that awareness into action. Letting go isn't just

The Organized Teacher Toolkit

a mindset—it's a skill you can practice and strengthen. Here's a simple plan to help you start small, build momentum, and make "letting go" part of your weekly routine.

1. *Audit Your Week:* For five days, track anything that feels like a time-waster, energy drain, or unnecessary stressor.

2. *Categorize Each Item:* Label it physical (clutter), mental (shoulds), or emotional (can't control).

3. *Choose One Small Release:* Don't overhaul everything at once; simply pick one thing from each category to let go this week.

4. *Schedule Maintenance:* Put a 15-minute "let it go" block on your weekly calendar to keep clutter, commitments, and thoughts in check.

5. *Celebrate the Wins:* Notice how much time or energy you free up when you release even small things.

Examples of "Let It Go" in Action

- *Grading Shift:* Instead of marking every single homework problem, grade only a sample set for accuracy and check the rest for completion, which will cut grading time in half.

- *Email Boundaries:* Reply to non-urgent parent emails during your two daily email blocks instead of on-demand, gaining back uninterrupted teaching time.

- *Committee Cutback:* I challenge you to step down from a volunteer committee that doesn't align with your priorities, opening up an afternoon per month for planning.

Tips for Making "Let It Go" Stick

- *Use "Stop-Doing" Lists:* Each month, list one to two things you'll stop doing because they aren't essential.

- *Pair Letting Go with Gains:* Every time you release something, decide how you'll use the time or energy you free up like eating lunch without multitasking or leaving school on time.

Time Management: Work Smarter, Not Harder

- *Have a Replacement Habit:* Instead of dwelling on something you can't control, replace it with an action you can take (e.g., instead of worrying about the online grading system going down, prep tomorrow's materials instead).

If you've always been the "yes" person or the over-preparer, letting go can feel like slacking off. But letting go is not neglect, it's strategy. The things you release create space for you to be more present, creative, and effective where it matters most. Your students benefit more from an energized, focused teacher than from a perfectly curated bulletin board or a 24/7 email responder. When you feel the urge to hold onto something—whether it's a stack of outdated worksheets, an unrealistic expectation, or frustration over something you can't change—say to yourself:

"Not everything is mine to carry."

This small reminder will help you pause, evaluate, and choose intentionally before you commit your time or energy.

The Let It Go Method is a time management strategy disguised as self-care. By letting go of what's unnecessary, you make your workload lighter, your decisions faster, and your teaching more focused. You also model to your students that it's okay to prioritize what matters most and release what doesn't serve you. Teaching will always come with more tasks than time. But you get to decide which ones you hold onto. And when you let go of the rest, you'll find not just more time, but more peace.

Now that you've discovered several new systems to help you manage your time, it's time to pick just one to two to put into action.

Task: Write down what's possible for you when you consistently use one to three systems from this chapter. Think about how you'll feel and what sort of things you'd say to yourself.

exxxistence/
Adobe Stock Photo

Chapter 5

Why Classroom Clutter Happens

You know how important managing your time is as a teacher, which is why you can probably relate to this challenge that so many teachers face. A few years ago, I walked into my classroom one Monday morning, vanilla chai in hand, ready to start the week. Except, before I could even take attendance, I realized I couldn't find the stack of math assessments I'd graded over the weekend. I checked my desk. I checked the counter. I checked the pile of "important papers" by my computer, and then the pile of "really important papers" on the kidney table. Ten minutes later, I found them buried under a stack of photocopies I'd never used from the week before.

Ten minutes might not sound like much, but in a teacher's world, as you know, it's the difference between starting the day calm and starting the day frazzled. Multiply that by a school year's worth of lost papers, misplaced books, and missing assignments, and you've got hours, sometimes even weeks, of lost time.

Our brains like order, and constant visual reminders of disorganization drain our cognitive resources, reducing our ability to focus. Research shows there is a direct correlation between productivity and clutter.[1] Productivity declines when clutter and chaos rise. In the business world, the National Association of Professional Organizers has found that paper clutter is the number one problem in

How many times has this happened to you?

---

[1] McMains, S. A., & Kastner, S. (2011). Interactions of top-down and bottom-up mechanisms in human visual cortex. *Journal of Neuroscience,* 31(2), 587–597. https://doi.org/10.1523/JNEUROSCI.3766-10.2011.

most workplaces, costing the average person 4.3 hours per week searching for misplaced items. That's more than 225 hours every year spent digging through piles instead of doing the work that matters most. And here's the thing, if that's true for the average office worker, imagine how much more it applies to teachers.

You don't just have paperwork; you have multiple *types* of paperwork from lesson plans, student work, assessments, IEP documentation, copies for the week, meeting notes, permission slips, substitute plans, and a constant influx of memos and forms from the office. On top of that, there's curriculum materials, manipulatives, classroom library books, seasonal decorations, and "just in case" supplies you've been holding onto for years (see Figure 5.1).

When you combine the sheer volume of stuff in a classroom with the fast pace of the school day, the time wasted looking for missing items can easily double or triple what the average worker experiences. And that lost time isn't just an inconvenience; it comes at the expense of your planning periods, your after-school hours, and ultimately your ability to leave school on time.

Figure 5.1 This classroom clutter is my former teacher workspace before the end of the day

Here's some real talk:

No matter how many organizing systems you put in place, they won't work if you have too much stuff. Systems can't organize excess, they just rearrange it.

And when you're surrounded by clutter, it's like carrying a mental load you can never put down. It makes it harder to think clearly, focus on your priorities, and leave school on time.

The solution isn't just "get organized." The real solution is to create a clutter-free classroom where your systems can thrive. When your environment is streamlined, your routines work better. You can find what you need when you need it, your students can be more independent, and you can walk into your classroom each day with a sense of calm instead of chaos.

And here's the best part, you don't have to do it all at once. In this chapter, I'm going to show you why your physical space matters and walk you through exactly how to declutter your classroom in a way that's simple, strategic, and actually doable in a real teacher's life. We'll talk about the common objections that keep us holding onto stuff, how to get started with quick wins so you see results right away, and then how to work through every area of your classroom without getting overwhelmed.

Common Objections That Keep Teachers Stuck

If it were as simple as me telling you to get rid of your stuff, you'd do it. As humans, we often form a deep emotional connection to our "stuff." Every resource, book, or set of manipulatives feels like a potential lifeline for a future lesson or student. This belief, that more materials automatically make us better prepared, can keep us stuck in a cycle of collecting and keeping far more than we actually use. Over time, these good intentions can backfire, creating overcrowded spaces where the truly useful tools get buried under layers of "someday" items. The irony is that the more we hold onto, the harder it becomes to find and use the things that actually help us teach. I'm curious if you can relate to Jessica's story below about why she holds on to all of the stuff in her classroom.

What part of Jessica's story resonates with you the most?

Did you know that letting go of what you don't use isn't wasteful; it's an act of respect for your time, your students, and your own well-being. It took me many years to recognize this. I can't tell you how many classroom moves I made where I kept packing and unpacking the same file of transparencies of my favorite matter lesson I created during student teaching although I hadn't used an overhead projector in years.

Since a cluttered space actually makes your job harder, let's change that and get clear on your beliefs about your stuff so that it's easier to get rid of things and so they don't pile up again.

If you think about what you've got tucked away in your files and cabinets, what would be the most shocking thing you'd find?

"I Don't Have Time."

If you're like most teachers, time is your scarcest resource. When the idea of decluttering comes up, it's natural for your brain to embrace the belief: *"I don't have time."* On the surface, that thought feels true. After all, there are always tasks that feel more urgent like finishing tomorrow's lesson plans or catching up on grading that seem to demand your

The Organized Teacher Toolkit

attention first. But here's the thing: clutter is already stealing your time in invisible ways. Not only is it draining your energy, but it's also costing you minutes and even hours every single week. And those minutes add up to days and weeks over the course of a school year.

According to a report cited by *Western Mass News*,[2] Americans spend about 17 hours per year searching for misplaced personal items like keys, phones, or glasses. That breaks down to roughly 16 minutes every time something goes missing. Think about how often you've spent those same 16 minutes in your classroom: hunting for the right math manipulatives, tracking down a book a student swore they returned, or searching through a pile of papers to find one critical form. Every minute spent searching is a minute lost from teaching, connecting with students, or simply taking a deep breath.

Teachers face a double whammy since clutter not only eats away at your own efficiency, but it also disrupts instruction. How many times have you stopped a lesson to look for dry-erase markers that actually work, or stopped mid-activity because you can't find the anchor chart you planned to make with your students? Those disruptions chip away at momentum and attention, not just for you but for your students as well. A study published in the *Journal of Neuroscience* found that when multiple visual stimuli are present, they compete for neural representation, which makes it harder for the brain to focus on what matters.[3] When your classroom is cluttered, both you and your students are more prone to distraction, which drags lessons out longer than necessary. What looks like a "time saver" by skipping decluttering is actually a time thief in disguise.

There's also the hidden cost of decision fatigue. Every time you sift through a pile, you're forcing your brain to make tiny choices: "Is this the right paper? Where should I put this? Do I need this now or later?" Decision fatigue is a well-documented

---

[2] Merten, Paxtyn. (2024, August 22). *Forgetting something? These are the most frequently lost items in America.* Western Mass News. https://www.westernmassnews.com/2024/08/22/forgetting-something-these-are-most-frequently-lost-items-america/.

[3] McMains, S. A., & Kastner, S. (2011). Interactions of top-down and bottom-up mechanisms in human visual cortex. *Journal of Neuroscience,* 31(2), 587–597. https://doi.org/10.1523/JNEUROSCI.3766-10.2011.

phenomenon where the more small decisions you make, the less mental energy you have for bigger, more important ones. For teachers, that means clutter is silently draining your capacity to make instructional decisions, manage behavior, or problem-solve creatively.

In other words, clutter isn't just costing you time—it's costing you brainpower.

So let's flip the limiting belief on its head: the very fact that you "don't have time" is *exactly* why you need to declutter. Think of it as a time investment rather than a time expense. Yes, spending 20 minutes decluttering a supply drawer might feel like a sacrifice today, but it will save you 5 minutes every day afterward when you don't have to rummage around for what you need. Over the course of a year, that's 15 hours of teaching time reclaimed just from a single drawer. Now multiply that by how many years you've been teaching or plan to teach and you can easily see that the payoff is enormous. Especially since clutter builds quietly until it starts to weigh on you. UCLA's Center on Everyday Lives of Families[4] found that women who described their homes as cluttered had consistently higher cortisol levels—the stress hormone—throughout the day. I'd imagine that women feel the same way about their classrooms and that stress shows up as irritability, fatigue, and a constant sense of being behind. Decluttering doesn't just save time, it reduces the mental load that's silently exhausting you.

I know that when you're juggling grading, lesson prep, and student needs, it feels easier to push off decluttering until "later." But "later" never comes. Instead, you end up in what psychologists call the "urgency effect"—focusing on tasks that feel immediately

---

[4] Saxbe, D. E., & Repetti, R. (2010). No place like home: Home tours correlate with daily patterns of mood and cortisol. *Personality and Social Psychology Bulletin,* 36(1), 71–81. https://doi.org/10.1177/0146167209352864 (original work published 2009).

pressing while ignoring important but not urgent ones. Decluttering falls into that second category: it won't scream at you to get it done today, but the long-term benefits are far more valuable than the short-term fires you're putting out.

And here's the part most teachers don't realize: decluttering also saves time for your students. A classroom that's organized allows students to find materials quickly, return them easily, and work independently without constant interruptions. That independence translates into fewer questions like "Where are the scissors?" or "Do we have any more glue sticks?" Over a year, those micro-interruptions add up just like yours do. Decluttering isn't just about you, it's about creating a smooth, efficient learning environment for everyone in the room.

At the heart of it, the belief "I don't have time to declutter" comes from a place of exhaustion and survival. And that's valid—you're carrying more than ever as an educator. But the truth is, clutter is part of the problem, not a separate task on top of it. Every step you take to reduce clutter is a step toward gaining back time, focus, and calm. The question isn't whether you can spare the time to declutter; it's whether you can afford to keep losing time to clutter.

"What If I Need This One Day?"

This is one of the most common and most convincing stories we tell ourselves as teachers. After all, you might have that one student who needs the specific worksheet you found at a conference 12 years ago, or the class set of copies you still have when you taught 1st grade three years ago, or that science kit you've been holding onto "just in case." But be honest, how many "just in case" items have you actually used in the past year? The reality is, most teachers in your building have supply closets that look more like mini storage units than functional teaching spaces. If you haven't touched it in over a year, it's likely taking up space you desperately need for things you actually use. Letting it go doesn't mean you're unprepared; it means you're making room for the tools and materials you reach for every day.

Why Classroom Clutter Happens

Real Teacher Talk

It is extremely hard for me to get rid of school stuff. I have been teaching for 44 years and moved across the country hauling all this school stuff! The reason is because when I first started teaching my classroom was rather bare and the school, system, state, or whoever gave very little funding. School teaching materials are EXPENSIVE! So as we could afford it, I purchased no consumable materials but materials that would last for years. Additionally if we moved to a different school or left the district, whatever was purchased with "school money" had to stay in that classroom. Not knowing what the next room would be like, full or bare, I didn't want to start all over with nothing. Over the years some great materials are no longer available. I have stored, moved, and hauled all these school materials around the country to 4 different states, 7 different systems, and 14 different classes and multiple grades! Teachers have and are at the mercy of where the administration wants to place them from year to year. I saved and stored so I would be prepared and have what I needed to start a new class or to use again because it was a valuable resource. I would not have to repurchase, saving personal money. You just never know what you are going to need. —Beth H.

"But I Spent Money On It!"

Oh, I have been there. You spent your own hard-earned money on that set of task cards or those adorable bulletin board borders, and it feels almost disrespectful to get rid of them, especially because you really shouldn't have to be funding your own classroom, when in reality, you should be paid a lot more. But here's the thing, keeping something you don't use won't get your money back. In fact, it's costing you in other ways: space, time, and mental energy. This is the sunk cost fallacy in action, holding onto something because of what you've already invested, even if it's no longer serving you. Instead, think of it this way: by letting go, you're creating space for tools that actually help you teach and run your classroom smoothly. And if the item is still in good condition, you can pass it along to another teacher who will use it, turning your purchase into a gift instead of clutter. And in the future when you're strolling the aisles of your favorite store, ask yourself, "Do I know exactly how I am going to use this?" before purchasing it.

"I'm Too Attached and It Holds Sentimental Value."

Some things are harder to let go of because they carry emotional weight: your first class picture, the handmade card from a student, or that project that took you hours to create during your first year. Sentimental items matter. But when they start taking over your workspace, they can interfere with your daily flow and productivity. The key is to be intentional. Choose a few special items to keep, maybe display them in a small frame or dedicate a single box for keepsakes, and let the rest go. That way, the things that matter most get the spotlight they deserve, instead of being buried under piles of unrelated stuff. I'll share actionable suggestions later in this chapter about what you can do with some of these items.

"I Don't Know Where to Start!"

This one stops so many teachers in their tracks. You look around your room, see the overflowing shelves, the crowded cabinets, the mystery piles that have somehow multiplied since last year, and it's paralyzing. When everything feels important, it's impossible to know where to begin so it's easy to just let things pile up. That's exactly why I created the Organized Teacher Declutter Method. It's a simple, step-by-step process that breaks the job into manageable chunks, starting with the easiest, most visible wins so you can see progress right away. You don't need to tackle your whole classroom in one sitting; you just need a plan and a starting point. Once you get moving, the momentum will take over.

Quick Wins

Before we go deep into the big decluttering projects, I want you to experience the momentum of quick wins. Instead of one task at the end of the chapter, I've created small, manageable tasks you can knock out in under 15 minutes that make an immediate visual impact. I *intentionally* kept these tasks short and simple. Not because I don't think you can do more, but because

Ask yourself: Why is it important for you to feel empowered to declutter your classroom?

I know you're already doing *so much*. The goal is a quick win, one small shift that helps you feel just a little more in control. You can do these all at once or space them out and do one per day like I recommend to teachers inside The Organized Teacher Club; it's totally up to you!

Quick Win Task #1: Your Desk

exxxistence/
Adobe Stock Photo

We are going to tackle the top of your desk but I promise it's going to be really easy. And if you're not in your classroom right now, you can do this at home.

- Grab a bin or a box.

- Take *everything* off your desk and put it in the bin. Don't organize, don't sort; we're not doing that yet.

- Wipe down the surface if you can.

- And then? You can put back your computer and your trusty pen cup but that's it! Leave it empty. No picture frames, lamps, papers; you get the idea! Nothing goes back for the next 3 days, so set your alarm right now because for the next 72 hours, the top of your desk will be empty.

Now I know some of you are already thinking, "But Kristen, this feels too easy," or "What about all the papers? What if I lose something important?" or even, "I *need* that stuff to get my job done."

I hear you. Truly.

But we're not getting rid of anything, we're just *pressing pause* on the clutter. You're putting it in a safe spot so you can feel what it's like to work at a clear desk. That's all. And yes, it might feel uncomfortable at first. That's normal. But that discomfort? It's actually showing you just how overloaded your space and your mind have been. And don't worry, we'll deal with the box. We'll tackle the piles. I promise. But for right now, I just want you to *feel* the difference of having a desk that's clear, calm, and yours again (see Figure 5.2). These wins give you the confidence to tackle the bigger areas and help you see the payoff right away.

Figure 5.2 Experience the feeling of a clean desk for a few days (submitted by Connie Sanderson)

Quick Win Task #2: Just One Paper Pile

First, can we just take a moment to celebrate? You completed your first task, and that is *huge*. That clear desk energy? It's real. And you're feeling it already. If you haven't tackled Task #1 yet, it's not too late! Go back, and complete that quick task because these tasks build on each other, and I promise, it's worth it. Now, if you *did* complete Task #1, I want you to think back to how it felt walking into your classroom this morning. That breath of calm. That moment of, "Wait . . . is this what it's *supposed* to feel like?" That's the feeling we're chasing today too.

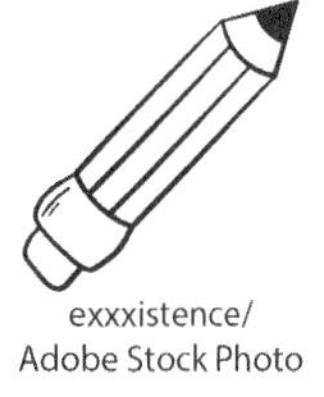
exxxistence/
Adobe Stock Photo

So let's talk about paper. I know, deep breath, right? Today's task is simple and should take no more than 10 minutes. Just like yesterday, I kept it short *on purpose*. Because I know if I told you to declutter *all* your paper, you'd either laugh or cry or maybe both.

Why Classroom Clutter Happens

So instead, here's what we're doing:

Find one paper pile. Not the whole box you cleared off your desk—that's for later. I'm talking about the one stack that's been sitting out staring at you. Maybe it's on your small group table, shoved in a turn-in bin, or stacked behind your doc cam. You know the one. And if you're at home, you also know what pile I'm talking about that's been sitting on your counter for weeks! That's your target for today and here's how to tackle it:

- Set a timer for 10 minutes.

- Sort that pile into three categories:

    1. Keep—stuff you *actually* need

    2. Toss or recycle—anything that's outdated, duplicated, or random

    3. Action—things that still need to get done (put these in a folder or tray labeled "To Do")

That's it. No overthinking. No making it perfect. It's what Connie S. did with her piles in Figure 5.3.

You're not trying to conquer paper once and for all; you're simply proving to yourself that paper clutter doesn't have to own you. And that's a powerful mindset shift. And if you want a little extra credit because you're on a roll:

- Declutter a second pile using the same three-step system

- Label your new "To Do" folder or tray and place it somewhere easy to access

- Glance through your inbox or teacher bag—if there's a mini pile of papers in there, give it a quick triage too

But only do this if you have the time and energy, and if not, you already did enough. If sorting this one pile made you realize just how much paper is floating around your classroom, you're not alone. This is where most teachers feel stuck. And it's exactly why I created systems inside The Organized Teacher Club to help you manage all of it—grading piles, lesson plans, copies, forms, you name it. The Club is full of

Figure 5.3 Before and after photo of a large paper pile being organized

plug-and-play systems that make it so much easier to keep paper under control without spending hours after school, and I'll be sharing more about these easily replicable systems with you in Chapter 11.

Quick Win Task #3: Pick Just One Shelf

You've cleared your desk. You've tackled that paper pile. And I know it might've felt *too* simple at times, but that's the whole point. These small wins? They build real momentum and I hope you're starting to feel it.

exxxistence/
Adobe Stock Photo

Now, we're heading to the shelves. Or the cabinets. Or the cubbies. Choose just one so you don't end up sitting in a massive pile of stuff three hours in, questioning all of your life decisions. Pick that one space that's been bugging you. The one you avoid opening, or the one that makes you think, "I'll get to that eventually."

Here's your task:

- Set a timer for 10 minutes.

- Take *everything* out of that space.

- Wipe it down.

- Sort that pile into two quick categories:

  1. Keep—stuff you *actually* need

  2. Toss or recycle—anything that's outdated, duplicated, or random

- Only put back what *you actually use* or *need to access*.

Quick Win Task #4: Revisit Your Desk

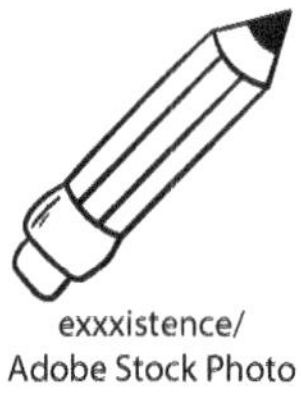

Now that it's been three days, let's visit the box from Task #1, but don't start this any sooner; that part's important! Pick just three to five items from the box that deserve a home in your newly decluttered space. You may be asking, why not put everything back? Remember how calm you felt while walking by your desk without seeing all of that visual clutter? That's why!

exxxistence/
Adobe Stock Photo

Here's a list of items you can consider keeping on top of your desk (see Figures 5.4 and 5.5):

- One or two pictures of your family

- One or two items that show your personality

- Cup with pens you use often (try to limit it to 10 pens max)

- Copy Clips with pen, highlighter, and whiteout tape

- Three-drawer system paper tray for copies (you'll learn more about that soon)

- Plant or lamp if possible

Figure 5.4   A before picture of a teacher desk area (submitted by Krystal F.)

Figure 5.5   An after picture of a teacher desk area (submitted by Krystal F.)

Why Classroom Clutter Happens

- On a small bulletin board near the desk, include student photographs. Every year, put those into an envelope and start fresh with a new group. Don't waste bulletin board space if you have a larger area above your desk. Use it for your students instead of posting student notes, etc.

- Computer

And if something in the box doesn't have a home yet? It's actually great information—it's showing you where you might need a better system. Sort it too. Keep, toss, or action; it's that simple. We're not leaving piles behind. I told you we'd get there!

You've already made real progress with these four quick tasks. You've cleared space. You've created calm. You're showing yourself what's possible when you give yourself *just a little* room to breathe and let go of your limiting beliefs around your stuff.

Chapter 6

Your Classroom Clutter Blueprint

Those quick wins are just the beginning. Now that you've had a taste of what's possible when you remove the extra "stuff" stealing your space and attention, it's time to go deeper. This is where you get to stop putting out small fires and start creating a classroom environment that works for you, not against you. How does that sound?

The Organized Teacher Declutter Method will walk you through every major area of your classroom, step-by-step, so nothing is left overwhelming you in the corner (or shoved into a cabinet "for later"). You'll learn exactly how to make decisions about what stays, what goes, and how to organize what's left so it supports your teaching and your students' learning.

We'll tackle each space one at a time, your classroom supplies, class library, teacher desk, small group area, cabinets, closet, filing cabinet, digital files, and learning centers, breaking the work into manageable pieces so you never feel buried. By the time you finish, you'll have a clutter-free classroom that feels calm, intentional, and ready for anything the school year throws at you. And the best part, in the next chapter, you'll uncover organization systems that will help you maintain your newly decluttered space.

Using the Organized Teacher Declutter Method

It doesn't have to be complicated and the items you need to make it possible are things you most likely already have. All you need to do is gather the following:

- *Big black trash bags*—for anything headed straight to the dumpster.

- *A big box*—for items that belong somewhere else in your classroom or school.

- *Keep/Toss/Action labels*—so decisions are clear and quick (see Figure 6.1).

- *A Time Timer*—to keep you focused and on track.

Figure 6.1   Keep/Toss/Action labels to keep you organized

- *Music*—because everything is more fun with a soundtrack. I even curated a Declutter playlist you can access when you click on the QR code in this book!

That's it. Seriously. I told you it would be easy!

Step-by-Step

1. Clear the obvious trash.

2. Grab your trash bag, set your timer, turn on some music, and quickly walk through the area picking up anything that's clearly garbage or broken.

3. Empty the space.

4. Get *every single item* in the area into one big pile—yes, *every* item. The only exception is large classroom furniture.

5. Group like items together.

6. Sorting by category helps you see when you have multiples (like the 14 pairs of scissors you didn't realize you owned).

7. Make decisions, one item at a time.

8. Pick up each item and decide:

- Keep—You use it often and it belongs in this space.

- Toss—It's broken, expired, or unusable, then put in the black trash bag.

- Action—This pile is for the things that you need to take action on and can even be divided into items that belong in another part of your classroom and items that are in good condition and need to be *easily* donated. The items that belong in another part of your classroom or school go in the big box.

You may be wondering, how do you know what to toss when you want to keep everything? The decision-making flow map shown in Figure 6.2 will help you take the guesswork out of it and remove any emotion so you can make this process faster.

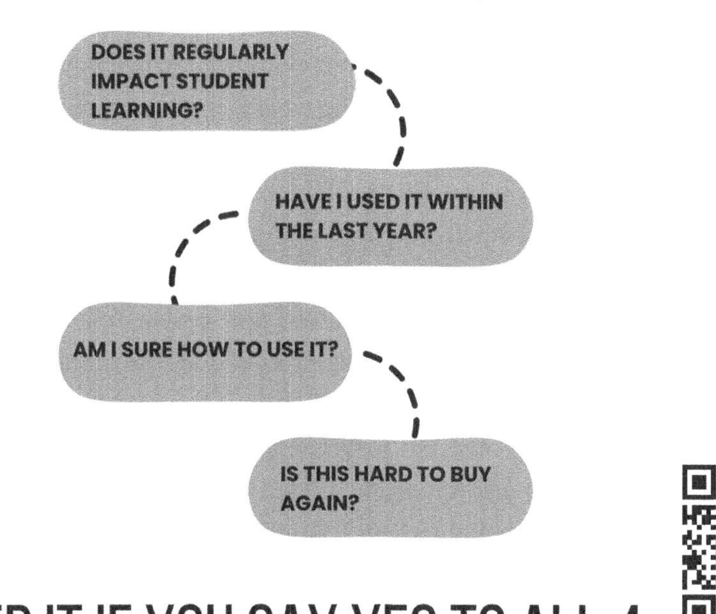

Figure 6.2   Decision-making flow map to help you decide what to keep

9. Clean Before You Return Items.

10. Wipe down all surfaces, shelves, and drawers before you put anything back.

11. Put Everything in Its Place:

- "Keep" items go back neatly into this space.

- "Action" items from the box get put away and the rest go in your donation area.

- "Toss" from the black trash bag goes in the dumpster.

12. Celebrate Your Win.

13. You just completed an area, and that's a big deal! Take a moment to appreciate the difference.

If you want more guidance on what exactly to do in each area of your classroom, I'll show you how to declutter those spaces step-by-step next.

Teacher Supplies

Your teacher supplies are often the most hidden clutter. They live in your desk drawers, filing cabinets, and personal shelves. Over the years, these spaces have become the catch-all for plan books, sticky notes, pens, paper clips, binders, and "teacher tools" you think you might need someday. The problem? When you're surrounded by outdated or broken materials, it slows you down and adds stress you don't even realize you're carrying.

Teacher supplies should make your life easier, not harder. When everything has a clear place and is in good condition, you save time, reduce frustration, and can focus your energy on planning and teaching. But when supplies are cluttered and chaotic, they actually become one more obstacle between you and your students.

Cluttered teacher supplies also create a hidden mental load. That drawer full of broken pens or old plan books might seem harmless, but every time you see it, your brain registers it as an unfinished task. It whispers: *"I should deal with that one day."* Over time, those "shoulds" pile up and contribute to decision fatigue.

Here's how to apply the Declutter Method specifically to your teacher supplies

1. Clear the Obvious Trash:

Start with the items that are easy to let go of: dried-out pens and highlighters, broken staplers or scissors, sticky note pads with two sheets left, or paper that's so wrinkled and faded it's unusable. These items aren't helping you and are just taking up valuable space.

Examples of what to toss:

- Old plan books (except for last year's) and grade books

- Outdated teacher's editions you no longer use

- Extra stamps you'll never get through (keep only 5–10 boxes max)

- More than two boxes of paper clips or binder clips

- Broken tape dispensers, staplers, or scissors

2. Empty and Sort:

Empty out your desk drawers, supply caddies, or shelves where these items live. Group like items together—pens with pens, sticky notes with sticky notes, paper clips with paper clips. You'll probably be surprised at how many duplicates you've accumulated.

3. Make Decisions, One Item at a Time:

Ask yourself:

- Do I use this regularly?

- Do I already have more than enough of this?

- Is this in good condition?

Be honest. You don't need seven tape dispensers or a decade of old grade books and plan books. Yes, I'm talking to you, because I was you and held onto all of my plan books for sentimental reasons!

Your Classroom Clutter Blueprint

4. **Keep Only What Serves You Now:**

Keep one working stapler, one or two pairs of scissors, two boxes of paper clips, a few fresh highlighters, pens that actually write, and a current plan book. Let the rest go. Remember: teaching is demanding enough without managing excess stuff.

5. **Clean and Reset:**

Before returning supplies, wipe down the inside of your drawers and organizers. Then set items back in a way that makes them easy to grab. Use drawer dividers or small bins if it helps.

6. **Maintain a System:**

- Limit how many extras you allow in your space. If someone offers you more paper clips and you already have two boxes, say no or pass them on.

- Set a reminder on your calendar or in your phone so at the end of each quarter, do a quick sweep of your drawers. Toss the broken pens that have crept in, recycle the outdated forms, and reset your supplies.

Practical Tips for Desk-Friendly Systems

Decluttering your teacher supplies isn't just about getting rid of extras—it's about setting up a system that makes your daily routines smoother. Here are a few ideas:

- **Streamline your desk:** Keep only the essentials within arm's reach: a few pens, sticky notes, and paper clips. Store backups in a nearby drawer or cabinet.

- **Create a "teacher-only" drawer:** This is where you keep the things you don't want students borrowing like your personal scissors, stapler, or nice pens.

- **Use clear containers:** When you can see what you have, you avoid overbuying or hoarding extras.

- **Set limits:** Decide in advance how many of an item you'll allow yourself (for example, no more than two tape dispensers). When you hit that limit, you don't keep more.

- **Create a tool box:** This can include common supplies that are used and easily accessible to you like Organized Teacher Club member Sabrena B did (see Figures 6.3 and 6.4).

Figure 6.3   A before photo of supplies being organized

Figure 6.4   A photo of a teacher tool box

Decluttering your teacher supplies may seem like a small thing, but it's incredibly freeing. Imagine opening your desk drawer and finding exactly what you need without rummaging through dried-out pens or broken clips. Imagine not feeling guilty about the stack of old plan books staring at you every day. Imagine a workspace that feels

Your Classroom Clutter Blueprint

clear, simple, and ready to support you. The difference is immediate. You'll waste less time. You'll feel calmer. And you'll notice how much more energy you have for the parts of teaching that truly matter.

Teacher Desk

Your desk is the command center of your classroom. It's where lesson plans come together, papers are graded, and a thousand little tasks get done in between. It's also one of the first places clutter likes to settle. Papers pile up, personal items accumulate, and before long, your desk feels less like a workspace and more like a dumping ground.

Real Teacher Talk

The area around my desk piles up the quickest. For some strange reason I can't just put something away if it doesn't have its designated spot. So I put it at my desk thinking I will fix a place. Time and decision frustrations interfere. I "overthink" it. What's the best place so I will remember where I put it? Trying to stay focused and on task is difficult because I feel so overwhelmed with the piles. —Beth H.

Here's the problem: when your desk is cluttered, it sends two messages—one to you, and one to your students. To you, it whispers stress: every pile represents something unfinished. To your students, it signals that clutter is acceptable, and if your desk looks chaotic, it becomes harder to hold them accountable for their own organization. Your desk is where your day begins and ends. If you arrive in the morning to a cluttered desk, it sets a tone of chaos before the first bell even rings. If you leave at the end of the day with piles staring back at you, it makes it hard to mentally disconnect from school.

Here's How to Apply the Declutter Method to Your Teacher Desk

1. **Clear the Surface.**

   Start by removing *everything* from your desktop. Yes, everything. The computer, the stacks of papers, the coffee mug collection, clear it all off so you're starting with a blank slate.

2. **Empty the Drawers.**

   Just like you did with student and teacher supplies, take everything out of your desk drawers. Group items by category: office supplies, personal care items, snacks, random extras.

3. **Make Decisions.**

   Use your four categories: keep, toss, donate, or move elsewhere. If you don't use it regularly, it doesn't belong on or in your desk.

   Keep inside your desk:

   - A small, limited set of supplies (sticky notes, paper clips, binder clips, correction tape).
   - A few personal care items: think toothbrush, deodorant, lotion, mints, or pain relievers.
   - Healthy snacks and a phone charger.

   Keep on top of your desk:

   - A cup with pens you actually use (limit to 10).
   - A copy clip with a pen, highlighter, and whiteout tape.
   - A three-drawer system or paper tray for copies.
   - One or two personal photos or small décor items.
   - A plant or lamp if it brings you joy.

   Everything else? Toss, donate, or move to a more appropriate storage spot.

4. **Clean and Reset.**

   Wipe down your desk surface and drawers. Then return items in a way that's both functional and inspiring. Essentials should be within arm's reach, backups tucked neatly away.

5. **Create a Personal Touch.**

   Your desk should feel like yours. One or two family photos, a small plant, or a student-made note are enough to personalize the space without overwhelming it.

Practical Tips for Desk-Friendly Systems

Decluttering once is powerful, but maintaining it is what creates lasting calm. Try these simple systems:

- **End-of-day reset.** Before you leave, clear your desk surface. Put papers in the tray, cap your pens, and leave your space ready for tomorrow.

- **Weekly sweep.** Spend five minutes on Friday tossing broken supplies, removing extra papers, and refreshing your space.

- **Limit décor.** A couple of personal touches are great. A dozen trinkets become clutter.

   Separate student vs. teacher items. Keep your desk a teacher-only zone. Student supplies should have their own clearly designated space elsewhere.

Your desk is your professional home base. It deserves to be treated with the same care and intentionality you bring to your teaching. Every item you keep should earn its spot by being useful, meaningful, or uplifting. Everything else is just noise.

Small Group Area

With your desk cleared and your command center reset, it's time to shift your focus to one of the most high-traffic, high-impact spaces in your classroom: the small group area. This is where so much of the real learning magic happens, reading groups, math practice, interventions, and one-on-one support. But it's also where piles of papers, broken supplies, and half-used materials tend to collect. Let's clear out the clutter so your small group area feels inviting, functional, and ready to serve students instead of distracting them.

Here's How to Apply the Declutter Method to Your Small Group Area

1. Start by clearing away everything on and around your small group table. Yes, everything.

2. Stack the items in one spot so you can see the full picture of what has accumulated.

3. Then begin sorting.

Items to remove immediately include

- Dried-out markers
- Broken crayons
- Worn-out erasers
- Torn notebooks
- Outdated textbooks
- Dried-up glue sticks
- Broken scissors
- Blunt pencils
- Empty pens
- Broken rulers
- Worn-out folders
- Damaged binders
- Outdated handouts
- Old worksheets or unused copies
- Bent or torn incentive coupons
- Dried-up paint
- Old stickers or stamps that no longer work
- Random game pieces with missing parts
- Worn-out flashcards
- Broken whiteboard markers

- Chipped or broken student whiteboards

- Tiny pencils and erasers that no one uses

- Old posters or anchor charts (take a photo and store digitally if you want to save the idea)

- Broken storage bins or containers

Once the clutter is cleared, group the supplies you actually use during small group instruction. Keep only items in good condition and directly tied to your teaching. Outdated or incomplete materials create more frustration than support, so it is better to let them go.

Practical Tips for a Small Group System

Once you have decluttered, create a system that makes the space easy to maintain.

- Store the supplies you use daily in a small caddy or drawer near the table.

- Keep only one set of extra student supplies and replenish them from your classroom stash as needed.

- Resist the urge to use the small group area as a holding zone for papers or random extras. Have students turn in work to the turn-in basket.

- Build in a reset routine. At the end of each day, clear the table, return supplies to their containers, and recycle papers you no longer need. This quick habit prevents clutter from piling up again.

Now you can call a group of students to your table and begin instruction right away. There are no piles to distract you, and no broken supplies to frustrate your students. Your small group area feels calm, focused, and inviting like Amanda D.'s area in Figures 6.5 and 6.6.

Student Supplies

If there's one area in your classroom that can take on a life of its own, it's student supplies. They come from everywhere: family donations, the school supply list, colleagues cleaning out closets, and those random extras that seem to just appear out

Figure 6.5   A before picture of Amanda's small group area

Figure 6.6   An after picture of Amanda's small group area

Your Classroom Clutter Blueprint

of thin air. Add in the things left behind by students year after year, and suddenly your classroom is packed with bins, drawers, and boxes overflowing with "stuff." Some of it is useful, but a lot of it is broken, outdated, or simply not serving anyone. Plus, if you typically aren't given money to purchase supplies, it's easy to hang onto items for the future, right?

But here's the truth: student supplies are meant to support learning, not slow it down. When they're unorganized, they become one more daily frustration. You waste precious minutes hunting for a working marker. Students interrupt lessons because they can't find a glue stick that isn't dried up. And let's not forget the mental weight of knowing the chaos is waiting for you every time you open a drawer.

The good news? Tackling supplies is one of the easiest, most energizing places to start decluttering because there's rarely sentimental value tied to them. Once you clear out the excess and create a simple system, you and your students immediately feel the difference. Supplies stop being a barrier and start becoming a tool for smooth, focused learning.

Here's How to Apply the Declutter Method to Your Student Supplies

You already know the steps from the Declutter Method: grab your supplies, set a timer, and dive in. Here's how it looks specifically for student supplies.

1. Clear the obvious trash. Start with the no-brainers such as dried-out markers, pencils without tips, broken crayons, glue sticks that are rock hard. Be ruthless here. If it doesn't work, it's not worth your time or space. Toss it without guilt.

2. Empty and sort. Once the obvious trash is gone, take everything else out of bins, drawers, and caddies. Spread it on a table or desk so you can see it all. Then group items by category: pencils, markers, scissors, headphones, notebooks, etc.

3. Make decisions, one item at a time. Ask yourself:

   - Is this in good condition?

   - Do my students use it regularly?

   - Do I need this many?

   If the answer is no, it goes into the donate or toss pile.

The Organized Teacher Toolkit

4. Keep only the best. Limit yourself to the essentials: sharp pencils, working markers, a class set of scissors, updated notebooks, and technology that functions. Store a few backups, but not dozens. One or two extra chargers are enough, you don't need five.

5. Clean and reset. Before you put anything back, wipe down bins and organizers. Create a clean slate. Then return items neatly, grouping them so they're easy to grab and easy to put away.

6. Maintain a system. The goal isn't just to declutter once, it's to prevent the clutter from creeping back in. Designate a clear "home" for each supply. Label containers. Teach students where things go. And create a simple routine for checking supplies weekly so you stay on top of it.

Real Teacher Talk

All students don't come with all their supply list. Several come with nothing but a backpack. I want them all to have the same start and feel equal. Our janitor is the one who has called me out on all my stuff! Probably because he had to move it over the summer! I inherited several things when I started teaching in public school. At first I wasn't sure what I needed, so I kept everything . . . when he'd give me a hard time, I'd just say, "Relax! There's less for you to vacuum daily!" —Michelle O.

Practical Tips for Student Supply System

Decluttering is only half the work, the other half is creating a system that lasts. Here are a few simple strategies that keep supplies organized long-term:

- Student supply stations. Dedicate one clearly labeled area where students can grab what they need. The clearer the system, the fewer interruptions during lessons (see Figure 6.7). These work great at student tables. Consider including hand sanitizer to make lining up for lunch quicker, scissors, crayons, pencils, markers, glue sticks, expo markers, and whiteboard erasers. I cut pencil erasers in half and students placed them in the supply caddy as well.

Your Classroom Clutter Blueprint

Figure 6.7 A supply caddy that can be kept at all table groups

- Teacher-only backups. Keep a small drawer or box with extras that only you can access. When supplies run low, you can quickly restock without hunting.

- Weekly supply jobs. Assign a student helper to check markers, sharpen pencils, and toss broken items once a week. This tiny routine prevents the clutter from building up again.

- Container simplicity. Fancy organizers aren't necessary. A few labeled bins or cups are enough. The key is that everything has a home and they are spread throughout the classroom for easy access (see Figure 6.8). The figure also shows clipboards being housed in a large bucket that you probably already have in your classroom.

Imagine walking into your classroom tomorrow and knowing exactly where everything is. You open a drawer, and instead of a jumble of broken pencils and dried glue sticks, you see a neat row of sharpened pencils ready for student use. A student grabs

The Organized Teacher Toolkit

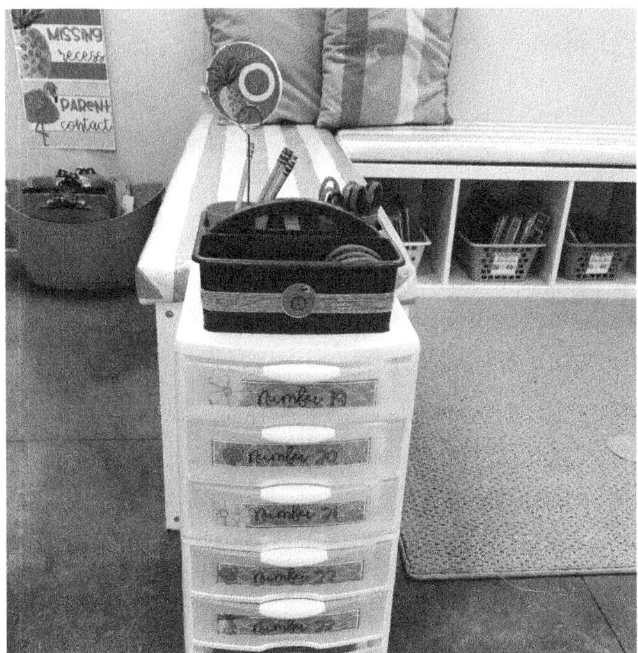

Figure 6.8 A supply caddy on top of drawers that hold student materials
Courtesy of Easy Teaching Tools, LLC

a marker and it actually works. Small details, yes, but they add up to a calmer, smoother, less stressful day.

Classroom Library

With your small group area reset and ready for learning, let's turn our attention to another high-impact space that often collects more than it should: the class library. Does your classroom library need a refresh? Maybe you have been collecting books for years and are running out of room. Or maybe you just started teaching and accepted boxes of donated books that seemed helpful at first but are now taking up more space than they are worth. Either way, it is easy for the class library to become cluttered, and when that happens, students stop using it the way you want them to. The goal is to have a library that feels inviting, organized, and full of books your students will actually read (see Figure 6.9). When you create that kind of space, the library becomes a highlight of your classroom instead of a source of stress.

Your Classroom Clutter Blueprint

Figure 6.9 My inviting classroom library
Courtesy of Easy Teaching Tools, LLC

Here's How to Apply the Declutter Method to Your Classroom Library

Follow the same simple steps you have been using in other areas of your classroom:

1. Remove all books from the shelves and wipe them down. Starting with a clean slate helps you see what you really have.

2. Assess the condition and relevance of each book. Remove any that are torn, missing pages, outdated, or no longer align with your teaching goals.

   a. Create a box of books to donate directly to students who do not have many at home.

   b. Donate the rest to your local library, Buy Nothing group, or community organization.

The Organized Teacher Toolkit

3. Sort the books that remain into categories that make sense for your classroom. You might organize them by fiction and nonfiction, by genre, by author, level or by theme. Use what you know about best literacy practices in addition to your school's preference. My school preferred using reading levels when the photo of Figure 6.10 was taken and if I were to do it again, I'd ensure the levels were not visible to students.

4. Return books to the shelves in a way that makes them easy to find and return. Labels, color-coded stickers, or baskets for primary grades can make a big difference.

> **Tip:** If you are unsure which books are actually read, try this simple trick. Place books with the spines facing out. When students return them, have them put the spines facing in. At the end of the year, the books that are still facing out are the ones no one picked up. This helps you make decisions about what to keep and what to let go of in the future.

Figure 6.10 Organized books in baskets

Courtesy of Easy Teaching Tools, LLC

Your Classroom Clutter Blueprint

Once the clutter is cleared, think about how you will keep your library fresh.

- Use clear labels and categories so students can return books independently.

- Rotate books seasonally or by theme to keep the shelves from feeling stagnant.

- Set up a donation or exchange shelf where students and families can bring in books they no longer use at home. This fosters a sense of community and helps your library evolve with your readers.

- Keep a small display area where you highlight student favorites, new titles, or featured authors to keep excitement high.

You will feel lighter knowing every book on your shelves is there for a reason. The library will stop being a source of stress and become a place you are proud to show off to administrators, families, and most importantly, your students. Now that your class library is refreshed and inviting, let's turn our attention to one of the most hidden yet overflowing spaces in many classrooms: the cabinets.

Cabinets

Cabinets are one of the easiest places for clutter to hide. Because the doors close, it is tempting to tuck away anything you are not sure what to do with. Over time, they become the catch-all for outdated materials, broken supplies, and random items that you might have forgotten about completely. Even though students may not see inside your cabinets, the clutter weighs on you every time you open the door or go searching for something.

Decluttering your cabinets is about turning them into a space that works for you. Instead of black holes filled with forgotten items, they can become efficient storage zones that actually make your teaching easier.

How many times have you shoved things into your cabinets just to get them out of the way?

Here's How to Apply the Declutter Method to Your Cabinets

Follow the same method you have been using in other areas of your classroom:

1. Empty one cabinet at a time. Do not try to tackle all of them at once. Place everything in a pile so you can see what has been hiding inside and wipe down the cabinet.

2. Toss or recycle anything that is broken, outdated, or incomplete. The first place to start is with your curriculum materials. These take up the most space and often linger the longest, even if you no longer use them.

Items to Remove Immediately Include

- Outdated books and curriculum guides

- Workbooks that have not been used in two or more years

- Broken manipulatives or manipulatives you have not touched in years

- Games that have missing pieces or that your students never use

If you hesitate, ask yourself: "Would I realistically use this with my current students?" If the answer is no, it is safe to let it go.

The second place to focus is the "junk cabinet." Every teacher has one. It is where random supplies, cords, and odds and ends tend to collect.

Items to Remove Immediately Include

- Dried-out pens and markers

- Old papers, notes, or receipts that are no longer needed

- Expired coupons or reward slips

- Broken or unused electronics such as calculators or chargers

- Old keys with no purpose

- Random cords and wires that do not match any current device

- Outdated or duplicate supplies like excess paper clips, rubber bands, or staples

Your Classroom Clutter Blueprint

- Empty containers that are just taking up space

- Unused or torn stationery such as bent paper clips or sticky notes with only a few sheets left

- Old snacks or food items past their expiration date

3. As you sort, keep reminding yourself: just because you have room does not mean you need to fill the space. Extra storage is not an excuse to hang on to clutter. Group the remaining items by category. Keep similar supplies together so you know what you have and can avoid unnecessary duplicates.

Return items to the cabinet in a way that makes them easy to find and access. Use bins, boxes, or even gallon bags to contain smaller items. Label everything clearly so there is no guessing later.

Practical Tips for Cabinet System

After decluttering, put systems in place to prevent cabinets from filling up again.

- Label bins and shelves so everything has a clear home.

- Store items by frequency of use. Daily items should be at eye level, occasional items can go higher or lower.

- Limit backstock. Keep one extra set of supplies if needed, but not more.

- Consider using a lid holder to organize your large construction paper, it's so helpful (see Figures 6.11–6.13).

- Do a quarterly sweep of your cabinets to make sure the clutter is not creeping back in and don't forget to schedule this reminder in your calendar or phone.

Imagine opening your cabinets and seeing neat, labeled bins with exactly what you need. You can grab materials quickly and return them just as easily. No more digging, no more buying duplicates, no more dreading what is behind the doors. Decluttering your cabinets creates hidden peace. With your cabinets cleared and streamlined, the next hidden storage zone to tackle is the closet.

Figure 6.11   Before photo of construction paper chaos

Figure 6.12   Organized construction paper you can easily grab

Figure 6.13 Organized cabinet

Classroom Closet

An organized closet can be one of your most valuable teaching tools. It can hold seasonal décor, personal items, or classroom backstock in a way that is neat, accessible, and stress-free. The key is to be intentional about what you allow to live there instead of it being a free-for-all.

Here's How to Apply the Declutter Method to Your Classroom Closet

1. Empty the closet completely. Taking everything out is the only way to see what is really hiding inside.

2. Sort items into categories and quickly remove anything that no longer belongs.

Items to Remove Immediately Include

- Broken umbrella, boots, or other weather gear
- Duplicate items you never use
- Dress-up day clothes you have not worn in two years
- Broken or outdated technology such as old projectors, computers, or audio equipment
- Empty or broken storage bins and containers
- Craft supplies that are dried out or no longer usable
- Broken furniture like damaged chairs, baskets, or flexible seating
- Expired cleaning supplies
- Old student work from previous years
- Unmatched items like single gloves or socks with no purpose
- Miscellaneous clutter that has not been used in over a year

3. Decide on a theme for your closet. Instead of letting it hold anything and everything, choose one primary purpose. For example, you might designate your closet as the home for personal items, or for seasonal decorations, or for larger supplies that do not fit elsewhere. Having a theme helps you stay consistent and avoid clutter creeping back in.

4. Return items neatly, using bins or labeled containers to keep categories clear. Store frequently used items at eye level and less-used items higher or lower.

Practical Tips for Closet System

After decluttering, create a system that will keep your closet intentional and functional.

Your Classroom Clutter Blueprint

- Stick to one theme for the closet to prevent it from becoming a catch-all.

- Store items in labeled bins so you can easily see what you have.

- Keep like items together so you do not waste time searching.

- Do a quick sweep each quarter to keep the space under control.

With a clear theme and simple systems, it becomes a space that supports your teaching instead of weighing you down. With your closet cleared and given a clear purpose, it is time to tackle one of the most dreaded but most freeing spaces of all: the filing cabinet.

Filing Cabinet

If there is one space almost every teacher dreads opening, it is the filing cabinet. Most are packed with mismatched class sets of copies, originals from student teaching days, outdated lesson plans, and more duplicates than you will ever use. Over time, the filing cabinet becomes less of a helpful resource and more of a paper graveyard.

The good news is that with a clear plan, you can transform your filing cabinet into a system that actually supports your teaching. Instead of wasting time digging through old papers, you will know exactly where to find what you need and feel confident letting go of what you do not. I challenge you to use just one filing cabinet.

Paper clutter is sneaky. Unlike broken markers or dried-out glue sticks, old papers often feel useful even when they are not. You tell yourself you might use them again, but the reality is that most papers sit untouched year after year. The more you keep, the harder it becomes to find the materials you actually need.

How many times have you filed away class sets of copies you didn't get to or even incomplete class sets so you'd have to make fewer copies next year?

A streamlined filing cabinet reduces stress, saves time, and keeps your teaching materials current. It also eliminates the guilt of holding onto years of papers you know you will never use.

Think about the brain power it takes to manage all of that!

The Organized Teacher Toolkit

Here's How to Apply the Declutter Method to Your Filing Cabinet

1. Decide whether you will tackle one drawer at a time or the whole cabinet. One drawer is usually best to avoid being overwhelmed.

2. Label your drawers by subject or theme to give the cabinet a clear structure. For example:

   - Drawer 1: Thematic activities

   - Drawer 2: ELA

   - Drawer 3: Math

   - Drawer 4: Science and Social Studies

Tip: Put the drawers you use least on the bottom to save your back!

---

3. Remove everything from one drawer and sort through each file, one item at a time. If you do all of your files at once, you most likely will get overwhelmed.

Items to Remove Immediately Include

- Any duplicates you do not need

- Lesson plans or curriculum materials that are more than 10 years old, unless you actively use them

- Outdated lesson plans, worksheets, or tests that no longer align with your current teaching

- Old student records that are past the required retention period

- Expired forms, notices, or permission slips

- Duplicate class sets of worksheets or partial class sets that take up space

- Irrelevant reference materials that do not support your current curriculum

- Printouts of emails, memos, or documents that are no longer needed

- Old assessments from previous years that you do not reference

---

Your Classroom Clutter Blueprint

- Anchor charts or student examples (take a photo, save digitally, and let the paper go)
- Ripped or worn-out file folders

4. Use fresh dividers to separate categories and make it easy to find what you need when printed on bright cardstock (see Figure 6.14).

5. Return only the files you truly use and keep them neat. Limit yourself to one copy of each item, you can always make new class sets when you need them.

Practical Tips for Filing Cabinet System

After decluttering, build a simple filing system you can maintain.

Scan to get this download

- Label each drawer by subject or theme.
- Use dividers for subcategories to avoid overstuffed folders.

Figure 6.14 File dividers to easily locate important files

- Keep only one original copy of a worksheet or lesson and recycle duplicates.

- Store digital versions of lesson plans, anchor charts, and student examples to cut down on paper. You can do this by snapping a photo and creating a photo album on your phone of anchor charts or student examples.

- Do a quick annual review to clear out outdated materials before the school year starts.

Now, you get to open your filing cabinet and see neatly labeled drawers with exactly what you need, and nothing more. Instead of dreading the mess, you feel confident and in control. With your filing cabinet finally streamlined and free of paper clutter, the next step is to tackle the digital version of the same problem: your computer files.

Google Drive

Just like your filing cabinet can become a paper graveyard, your Google Drive can quickly turn into a digital dumping ground. Every shared document, downloaded file, or lesson plan you created years ago lives there, often unorganized and forgotten. Over time, this clutter slows you down. You waste time searching for the right file, you lose track of updated versions, and you feel a constant low-level stress knowing your Drive is messy.

The good news is that digital clutter is easier to manage than paper clutter once you have a system. With a little intentional effort, your Google Drive can become one of the most powerful tools you have to save time and keep your teaching organized.

When your digital files are unorganized, you spend more time looking for things than using them. A study from McKinsey[1] found that the average worker spends nearly two hours a day searching for information. Teachers feel this even more because so much of our planning and communication now happens digitally.

A streamlined Google Drive means you can find what you need quickly, collaborate more easily with colleagues, and feel confident that your files are up to date. It also reduces the mental clutter of seeing a long, unorganized list every time you log in.

---

[1] Wills, B. (2024, November 5). Does your workforce spend too much time searching for information? ProProfs Knowledge Base. https://www.proprofskb.com/blog/workforce-spend-much-time-searching-information/.

Here's How to Apply the Declutter Method to Your Google Drive

1. Start with your main Drive view. Switch to a list view so you can see more files at once.

2. Create main folders to give your Drive a clear structure. For example:

   - *Categorize by purpose:* Set up main folders such as Lesson Plans, Student Work, Administrative Documents, Professional Development.

   - *Use subfolders:* Inside each main folder, add subfolders. For Student Work, create subfolders by class, grade level, or quarter. For Lesson Plans, create subfolders for each subject and then folders inside for each strand. Choose a system that makes the most sense for you. Some teachers prefer subfolders by unit, others by standard, or even by month. Keep it simple and consistent.

Tip: Place files you use least often in a separate folder so they do not clutter your main workspace.

---

3. Color-code folders. You can assign colors to easily distinguish categories at a glance.

4. Utilize Google Drive features

   - *Starred:* Star your most-used files and folders for quick access.

   - *Priority workspace:* Add key files so they surface at the top of Drive.

   - *Number Folders:* You can number your folders to put them in order from most important to least important if you'd like.

5. Go folder by folder. For each one, drag, drop, or delete files as needed.

Files to Remove Immediately Include

- Duplicate versions of the same file (keep the most updated one)

- Old student work or projects that are no longer needed

- Memos, emails, or notices that no longer serve a purpose

The Organized Teacher Toolkit

- Files that do not align with your current grade level or subject

- Outdated lesson plans or resources you no longer use. Consider deleting anything you haven't used in two years.

Tip: Quick way to surface old files: In My Drive, click the Last Modified column, choose last modified, then last modified by me, or last opened by me and you'll be able to see the last time it was accessed. Then, click the arrow to change sort direction, and use the three dots next to any file to move it to the trash.

Organizing Shared Google Drive

Organizing shared folders can be trickier since you do not control the original structure and your team most likely shares a lot of documents with you. These strategies keep your view tidy and usable.

Organize shared files. The "Shared with Me" section of Google Drive can be overwhelming, but you can move those files into your own organized folders. If you collaborate with a team, consider creating one shared team folder so everyone has access to current versions.

Deleting files from a shared Google Drive depends on your permissions. Here's how it works:

- *Owner:* If you are the owner of the shared folder or file, you have full control and can delete it.

- *Editor:* If you have edit permissions, you can delete files, but this action will affect all collaborators.

- *Viewer/Commenter:* If you only have view or comment permissions, you cannot delete files.

Deleting Files You Own

- *Navigate to File:* Go to the shared folder in Google Drive.

- *Right-Click:* Right-click on the file you want to delete.

115

- *Delete:* Select "Remove" from the context menu. The file will be moved to your trash.

Deleting Files Shared with You

- *Navigate to File:* Go to "Shared with Me" in Google Drive.

- *Right-Click:* Right-click on the file you want to remove.

- *Remove Shortcut:* Select "Remove" from the context menu. This action removes the file from your view, but it remains accessible to others.

Emptying the Trash

- *Go to Trash:* On the left-hand menu, click on "Trash."

- *Permanently Delete:* To permanently delete the file, right-click on it in the trash and select "Delete Forever."

Considerations for Shared Drives

- *Shared Drives:* In Shared Drives, all members with Content Manager access or higher can delete files.

- *Impact on Collaborators:* Deleting files from Shared Drives affects all members, so ensure the files are no longer needed by anyone.

Restoring Deleted Files

- *Within 30 Days:* Files in the trash can be restored within 30 days unless the trash is emptied.

- *Restore File:* Go to "Trash," right-click the file, and select "Restore."

By implementing these strategies, you can maintain a well-organized structure for the folders and files shared with you, making it easier to navigate and manage your Google Drive. But what about all of your digital files on your computer?

Digital Files on Your Computer

Just like your filing cabinet and Google Drive, your computer can quickly become a clutter magnet. Old downloads, random screenshots, and duplicate documents pile up until you can't find what you actually need. A little attention here goes a long way in saving time and reducing frustration.

Here's How to Apply the Declutter Method to Your Digital Files

1. Create main folders on your desktop. Set up broad Categories such as Lesson Plans, Student Work, Professional Development, and Personal.

2. Use subfolders and organize within those categories by unit, month, or project depending on what makes the most sense to you.

3. Rename files clearly. Use descriptive names with dates, like Reading_GroupPlans_ April2026.

4. Clear your desktop and move everything into the right folders. A clean desktop helps your computer run faster and keeps you focused.

5. Clean out your Downloads folder and delete duplicates and old files you don't need.

6. Archive or back up your files if needed. Move older but important files to an external drive or cloud storage.

7. Schedule maintenance. Set aside 10 minutes each month to delete unused files and keep things current. A great time to do this is during Specials when you have to be a warm body in the room but aren't actually teaching.

What to Delete Immediately

- Duplicate copies
- Outdated lesson plans
- Random downloads or screenshots
- Old student work no longer needed
- Incomplete files or notes you haven't touched in years

Your Classroom Clutter Blueprint

A tidy computer means less scrolling, less stress, and more time to focus on what matters.

Practical Tips for Digital Files System

Once you declutter, the key is to keep your Google Drive and computer organized moving forward.

- Create a "To File" folder where you temporarily drop new files. At the end of each week, take five minutes to sort them into the correct folder.
- Use consistent naming conventions so you always know what a file is without opening it. For example: "Math_Unit3_Fractions_Assessment."
- Keep shared files in designated team folders so you are not constantly digging through your "Shared with Me" list.
- Schedule a quarterly digital cleanup session to delete old files and keep your system fresh.

Decluttering your digital files is not just about saving space, it is about saving time and energy every single day. If you're wondering about those piles of paper on your desk or counter, don't worry, we're going to cover paper clutter in its own chapter where you'll discover proven organization systems. For now, focus on clearing the bigger storage areas so that when we tackle paper, you'll already have space and systems ready for it.

With your filing cabinets, digital files, and every major classroom space decluttered, you now have the foundation for a classroom that feels calm and manageable. To help you, or any new teacher start strong, here's a simple clutter-free checklist to guide your setup.

Clutter-Free Checklist for New Teachers

Starting your teaching journey is exciting, but it is also overwhelming. Classrooms often come packed with leftover items from previous teachers, and the temptation to over-buy can be strong. Use this checklist to help you begin clutter-free and focused on what truly matters.

Must-Have Essentials for a Clutter-Free Start

- Clear storage bins in small, medium, and large sizes
- A laminator
- A milk crate for storing student assessments and notes
- Basic teacher desk supplies (pens, scissors, sticky notes, colorful Expo markers)
- School-to-home folders for communication
- A student mailbox system for papers going home
- A daily bin or tray for copies and materials by subject
- A three-drawer paper system for weekly sorting
- A Time Timer for you and your students

Common Clutter Traps to Avoid

- Giant themed décor sets (add personality later, not all at once)
- More than 10 bins with no plan for what goes in them
- Bulk "just in case" supplies (like 500 popsicle sticks)
- Extra furniture that eats up floor space
- Old or broken technology
- Flexible seating (save this for after you've gained experience with your class)
- Brand new books (start small, build your library over time)
- Motivational posters (curate a few meaningful ones instead of covering every wall)
- Expensive games or gadgets from teacher supply stores

If You Inherit a Classroom Full of Stuff (Spoiler: Start Fresh)

- Adopt a clean slate mindset: remove old butcher paper, borders, or leftover decorations.
- Sort fast: create three piles—Keep, Donate, Toss.

Your Classroom Clutter Blueprint

- Be ruthless: if it is broken, outdated, or only "might be useful someday," let it go.

- Only keep what you would choose today: if you would not buy it yourself, don't keep it.

- Check with administration before discarding or donating school property.

- Respect sentimental items but prioritize function. Keep a treasure or two, not a museum.

- Make friends with the custodian. A little kindness (and snacks) can go a long way in helping you clear out what you do not need.

Decluttering your classroom is not about perfection or having everything match. It is about creating a space where you and your students can focus on learning without distractions. Every drawer you cleared, every outdated resource you recycled, and every system you put in place makes your teaching lighter and more sustainable. By taking the time to declutter, you are not just organizing things, you are reclaiming your time, energy, and presence in the classroom.

As you close this chapter, remember that clutter is never just about stuff, it is about the way your environment supports or hinders your best teaching. The systems you set up now will carry you through the year with more clarity and calm.

You've done the hard work of clearing the clutter and setting up simple systems. Now comes the fun part: deciding how to use the space you've created. Your classroom layout is more than where desks and shelves go; it's the story your room tells the moment someone walks in. A thoughtful layout supports learning, saves you time, and helps students feel calm and focused. With your space decluttered, you now have the freedom to be intentional about how every corner of your classroom functions.

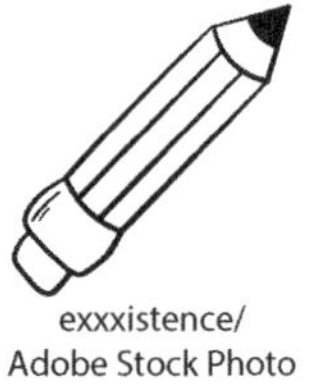

Task: Take a moment to reflect: *What is one small area of clutter I can clear today that will make tomorrow feel lighter?*

exxxistence/
Adobe Stock Photo

Chapter 7

The Physical Classroom Environment

As teachers, we spend so much time talking about lesson plans, curriculum pacing, assessments, and the latest teaching strategies. But let's pause for a moment and ask: what about the physical space where all of this learning takes place? Your classroom walls, your desk arrangement, the way supplies are stored, even the lighting; these aren't just background details. They're active players in how your students experience school, and they have a direct impact on your stress level, energy, and effectiveness as a teacher.

I know firsthand how an organized, thoughtfully arranged classroom can transform not only student learning but also the way you feel walking through that door each morning. Research continues to back up what many of us instinctively know: the physical environment of your classroom matters more than most people realize. In this chapter, we'll look at why the physical environment is so powerful, what the research says, and most importantly, how you can set up and maintain a space that truly works for you and your students.

Creating a Productive Learning Environment

Have you ever walked into a classroom that instantly made you feel calm, focused, and ready to learn? That's no accident, it's science! A productive learning environment isn't just about students working quietly at their desks. It's about crafting a space that invites focus, lowers stress, and sets the tone for learning.

Real Teacher Talk

My Environment score on the teacher evaluation was the highest score because everything was neat, organized, and structured. —Margaret M.

One of the best parts of teaching is that you get to create the atmosphere in your room. The way you set up your classroom communicates your expectations before you ever open your mouth. Students and adults pick up subtle cues: whether supplies are easy to find, whether there's space to move without bumping into things, whether the walls are cluttered or calm. If things feel unstructured and chaotic, students may reflect that same energy in their behavior and focus. But when the room is carefully planned and intentional, students walk in ready to meet those unspoken expectations with ease.

Research from Edutopia[1] notes that classroom environments aligned with learning objectives enhance both student morale and achievement. When the physical setup reflects purpose and clarity, students feel more invested. Organized classrooms also lead to more on-task behavior and improved academic performance, especially for students with special needs. According to the Indiana Institute on Disability and Community,[2] for example, structured environments are particularly helpful for children on the autism spectrum, reducing anxiety and helping them understand routines.

Think about your own experience: have you ever wasted five minutes digging for a stapler, or shuffled through piles to find that one copy you swear you just printed? Those aren't just annoyances, they're lost instructional minutes. Multiply that by a year, and you're looking at hours of wasted time. Creating a productive environment means setting yourself and your students up for success, so continue to ask yourself the following questions:

- What message is my classroom sending to my students right now?

- What is working really well?

- What small tweak could make it even better tomorrow?

---

[1] Phillips, M. (2014, May 20). A place for learning: The physical environment of classrooms. Edutopia. https://www.edutopia.org/blog/the-physical-environment-of-classrooms-mark-phillips.
[2] Indiana Institute on Disability and Community. (2020). *Clean up your Act: Creating an Organized Classroom Environment for Students on the Spectrum*. Indiana University Bloomington. https://iidc.indiana.edu/irca/articles/clean-up-your-act-creating-an-organized-classroom-environment-for-students-on-the-spectrum.html.

The Role of Physical Space in Learning

Physical space is more than just four walls. Lighting, color, acoustics, and layout all influence learning outcomes. Researchers from the University of Salford in the UK[3] studied 3,766 students across 153 classrooms and found that well-designed classrooms can boost academic progress by up to 25% in a single year.

Lighting

Lighting, for example, is critical. Did you know that natural light, in particular, has been linked to higher test scores, improved behavior, and reduced fatigue. Natural light boosts alertness and mood, while poor lighting is linked to lower engagement and even eye strain. If you're lucky enough to be in a classroom with natural light, take advantage of it. And if you're not, consider turning off the harsh fluorescent lights and see if your local Facebook Buy Nothing group can donate soft desk lamps to bring some warmth into your classroom. Think about how you feel under glaring lights in a conference room compared to working near a sunny window; your students experience the same effect.

Students need different levels of brightness depending on the task. For instance, bright lighting supports alertness during tests, while softer, warmer light can calm the room during reading time. Thoughtful adjustments help students regulate energy levels and attention throughout the day. Even if you don't have dimmers (because you don't even have control over your thermostat) or control over fixtures, you can still take steps to make your lighting more student-friendly.

Actionable Tips for Lighting

- *Maximize natural light:* Keep blinds or shades open during the day and avoid blocking windows with furniture, blinds, posters and anchor charts, and student work.

- *Use lamps or floor lights:* Add softer lighting in corners for reading areas or calming spaces. Consider putting them on timers or connecting all of them to a remote so you can have a student turn them on in the morning and off in the afternoon.

---

[3] Barrett, P., Davies, F., Zhang, Y., & Barrett, L. (2015). The impact of classroom design on pupils' learning: Final results of a holistic, multi-level analysis. *Building and Environment*, 89, 118–133. https://doi.org/10.1016/j.buildenv.2015.02.013.

- *Balance brightness:* Combine overhead lights with softer side lighting to reduce glare and shadows. I rarely turned on our overhead lights and always had them off after lunch to create a calm environment when students came in from lunch to help get them focused right away.

- *Control screen glare:* Angle desks and projectors so students aren't squinting at reflections on screens or whiteboards.

- *Create lighting "zones":* Use brighter areas for focused work and calmer, dimmer corners for independent reading or reflection.

Just as lighting sets the tone for your classroom, the colors you choose also influence how students feel and learn. Color can energize, calm, or even distract, making it one of the most powerful yet overlooked design choices in a classroom.

Color

Color choices can either energize or overwhelm. Color isn't just a design choice, it's a psychological tool that can either support or sabotage learning. Bright, bold colors can energize a space, sparking creativity and excitement. That's why you often see vibrant shades in early childhood classrooms, where play and exploration are central. But too much intensity such as walls covered in red, for example, can be overstimulating, raising stress levels and making it harder for students to settle into focused tasks. On the other hand, muted tones like soft blues, greens, and earth shades tend to promote calm and concentration, which can be especially helpful during independent work or testing. Avoid extreme colors such as black or neon green and opt for a pleasant mix of neutrals with pops of color.

The key isn't to strip your classroom of color altogether but to use it intentionally. Think about balance. For example, you might use pops of bright color to highlight interactive areas like a reading nook, math manipulatives, or an art station. Then, keep the majority of the room in calmer, more neutral tones so students don't feel overwhelmed. Another simple tip: use one consistent color scheme for bulletin boards and bins. This creates a cohesive look that reduces visual clutter while still adding warmth and personality to your classroom. If repainting walls isn't an option, consider colored borders, paper, or even fabric backdrops to bring intentional color choices into your space.

The Organized Teacher Toolkit

While color choices affect the overall energy and mood of your classroom, sound plays an equally powerful role. Did you know that acoustics show how well students can hear you and each other and they directly shape participation, focus, and even behavior? A room that looks inviting but sounds chaotic can still leave students struggling to learn.

Acoustics

While color shapes how students *see* the classroom, acoustics shape how they *hear* it, and hearing is directly tied to learning. Studies consistently show that poor classroom acoustics hinder participation and comprehension, particularly for English language learners, younger children, and students with hearing difficulties. Background noise, whether it's traffic outside, a noisy HVAC system, or even the hum of nearby classrooms, competes with your voice. When students can't hear instructions clearly, their brains expend more energy decoding sounds, leaving less cognitive capacity for actual learning. Over time, this leads to fatigue and disengagement. Shield and Dockrell[4] reviewed dozens of studies and found that noise significantly interferes with speech perception, reading acquisition, and memory, with younger students and second-language learners most affected.

Acoustics don't just affect comprehension, they influence equity. Klatte et al.[5] found that children in classrooms with poor acoustics not only scored lower on reading tasks but also reported higher levels of fatigue and frustration compared to peers in quieter environments. This shows that sound conditions directly affect both performance and well-being. Good acoustics ensure that *all* students, especially the most vulnerable, have equal access to learning. For teachers, improving sound quality also reduces strain on your voice, making daily instruction more sustainable and less exhausting.

---

[4] Shield, B. M., & Dockrell, J. E. (2003). The effects of noise on children at school: A review. *Journal of Building Acoustics*, 10(2), 97–116. https://doi.org/10.1260/135101003768965960.

[5] Klatte, M., Hellbrück, J., Seidel, J., & Leistner, P. (2010). Effects of classroom acoustics on performance and well-being in elementary school children: A field study. *Environment and Behavior*, 42(5), 659–692. https://doi.org/10.1177/0013916509336813.

Another way to shape the sound environment is through the intentional use of music. Playing calming background music as students enter the classroom can signal a shift from the chaos of the hallway to the focus of learning. Gentle instrumental tracks or nature sounds help lower stress and set a predictable routine that eases the transition into class. Many teachers find that this simple practice reduces chatter at the start of lessons and creates an inviting, calm atmosphere. The key is to choose music without lyrics and to keep the volume low so it enhances focus rather than competes with it. This is something I did every morning, when students came in from lunch, recess, or PE, and throughout the day to create a calm, peaceful environment.

Additional Actionable Steps for Acoustics

- Position strategically: Keep high-need students (English learners, those with hearing supports, or attention challenges) close to your primary teaching area and away from doors/windows.

- Use portable sound systems: If your district provides microphones or voice amplification, use them because it evens out sound for students at the back. Plus they are fantastic for your learners to speak into so that everyone can hear them!

- Rearrange furniture thoughtfully: Place bookshelves, soft seating, or fabric dividers along walls to reduce echo.

- Build "quiet corners": Create spaces in the classroom where students can step away from noise during independent work.

- Collaborate with facilities staff: If persistent noise (like HVAC hum or hallway echoes) is a problem, request basic adjustments like sound baffles or weather stripping around doors.

- Stream music without lyrics: check out "Rockabye Lullaby" and then add your favorite artist! You can hear all of your favorite music in lullaby form. Before streaming was a thing, I'd purchase these on CDs and play them on my CD player for my students!

Sound isn't the only sensory element that can overwhelm students, because what they see on your walls matters just as much. Just like noisy classrooms can make it hard

The Organized Teacher Toolkit

to concentrate, overly busy or underutilized walls can either distract students or leave the space feeling uninspired. That's why it's important to think intentionally about how you use your wall space.

Wall Space: Less Can Be More

One element of classroom design that often gets overlooked or overdone is wall space. Teachers sometimes feel pressure to cover every inch with posters, charts, and decorations, believing that more visual input equals more learning. But the opposite can be true. Research shows that overly cluttered walls can increase distraction and cognitive overload, especially for younger learners, while blank walls can feel sterile and uninspiring. The goal is balance. Think of your walls as valuable teaching real estate. Anchor charts should be made *with* students and reference tools should be purposeful and placed where students can actually use them. Student work should be displayed proudly and rotated regularly, so everyone sees themselves represented. Decorative touches can add warmth and personality, but they should never compete with instructional materials. Leaving intentional "white space" is just as important as what you put up because it gives students' eyes a place to rest and keeps the overall environment calm and focused.

I'll never forget walking into a colleague's classroom early in my career. She was one of those teachers who poured her whole heart into her room. She was a fantastic teacher who I learned a lot from but I remember so many of our Professional Learning Community (PLC) meetings were in her classroom and every wall was covered with posters: inspirational quotes, laminated phonics charts, addition facts, grammar rules, science diagrams, and Guided Language Acquisition Design (GLAD) charts. The ceiling had strings of laminated vocabulary words hanging down like mobiles. Her bulletin boards were stuffed with student projects, seasonal borders, and layers of papers from previous units. Even the cabinets and doors were covered in colorful butcher paper.

It was clear she wanted her students to feel surrounded by learning. Her intentions were good, and it was clear she didn't want to waste a single inch of space. But the moment you stepped into her classroom, it felt overwhelming and overstimulating. I remember thinking, *Where am I supposed to look?* The room was so busy, I couldn't focus on any one thing.

I'd imagine her students felt the same way based on what the research says. When I'd observe her teaching, her students often ignored the reference charts completely, not because they didn't need them, but because they couldn't tell which ones were relevant and weren't sure how to access them. When she introduced a new math anchor chart, it would just blend into the visual noise already plastered around the room. Some students even admitted they felt anxious sitting in that space, like there was "too much going on" around them.

The irony was that all of those resources were meant to *help* students, but instead they created confusion. Over time, at the recommendation of the fire marshal, she began to pare things back and started taking down the ceiling hangings, storing old anchor charts in a binder, and dedicating one wall to current references only. The difference in her classroom was immediate. Students actually began *using* the charts because they were visible and accessible. The space felt calmer, and she found herself spending less time redirecting distracted students. Sometimes less really is more.

Why Wall Clutter Matters

Have you ever walked into a classroom like that before and immediately felt overwhelmed?

What that teacher experienced isn't unusual. Research backs this up according to Fisher et al.[6] which found that children in highly decorated classrooms were more distracted and learned less than those in simpler spaces. The researchers concluded that while some visual stimulation is beneficial, too much can actually interfere with learning.

This connects directly to Cognitive Load Theory, which tells us that our working memory has a limited capacity for processing information and can easily become overloaded.[7] When students are bombarded with irrelevant

---

[6] Fisher, A. V., Godwin, K. E., & Seltman, H. (2014). Visual environment, attention allocation, and learning in young children: When too much of a good thing may be bad. *Psychological Science*, 25(7), 1362–1370. https://doi.org/10.1177/0956797614533801.

[7] Sweller, J. (1988). Cognitive load during problem solving: Effects on learning. *Cognitive Science*, 12(2), 257–285. https://doi.org/10.1207/s15516709cog1202_4.

visuals, their brains waste valuable energy filtering out distractions instead of focusing on the lesson. Researchers call this *extraneous load*, mental effort that doesn't contribute to actual learning.[8] The impact is even stronger for younger students or those with attention challenges, who have fewer strategies and coping skills for tuning out distractions. You've probably seen this in your classroom. Removing unnecessary visuals improves both attention and retention, which is essential for students when we're already competing for their attention. In other words, when it comes to your classroom walls, less really can mean more learning.

Practical Ways to Simplify

If you're worried your classroom walls are "too much," don't panic because you don't have to strip everything bare. Here are some practical strategies to help you make your walls work *for* you instead of against you:

1. Rotate Displays   Not everything has to be up at once. Keep current anchor charts on the wall and store older ones in a binder or on a ring that students can access if they need them. This keeps walls fresh and relevant.

2. Create Purposeful Zones for Walls   Dedicate one area for reference materials (word walls, anchor charts), one for student work, and one for decorative or seasonal elements. Keeping categories separate prevents clutter from blending together.

3. Use Consistent Borders and Colors   Too many competing colors and patterns create noise. Stick with one or two border styles and a simple color palette. This makes everything feel cohesive and less distracting.

4. Keep Student Work Central   Students should see their own work celebrated on the walls. Rotate projects regularly so everyone gets a turn. This builds ownership and pride while also keeping displays fresh.

---

[8] Paas, F., & van Merriënboer, J. J. G. (1994). Instructional control of cognitive load in the training of complex cognitive tasks. *Educational Psychology Review*, 6(4), 351–371. https://doi.org/10.1007/BF02213420.

The Physical Classroom Environment

5. Leave White Space It's okay to have empty spots. Blank spaces act like "visual rest areas," giving students' eyes and brains a break. Think of it like margins on a page, you wouldn't want to read a book without them.

6. Make Charts Interactive Instead of covering walls with static posters that hardly get used, turn reference materials into interactive tools like Velcro word walls, pocket charts, magnetic boards, or interactive charts with Post-it notes. This keeps displays purposeful because students *use* them, rather than just looking past them (see Figure 7.1).

Figure 7.1 A chart made with students that they refer back to

7. Go Seasonal with Purpose   Limit decorative displays to one small area of the room and tie them to current units or seasons. One way to easily do this is use thematic digital slides; student art can be seasonal and serve two purposes. This keeps the classroom feeling fresh without overwhelming students with too many competing visuals at once.

8. Think Vertical Storage, Not Display   Use walls for storage solutions like hanging file organizers or supply pockets rather than just decorations. A clear hanging shoe organizer works well to store math manipulatives. This reduces clutter on surfaces and ensures walls are functional as well as attractive.

9. Feature One "Big Idea" at a Time   Choose one anchor chart, essential question, or learning target to highlight each week. Frame it, spotlight it, or place it prominently. This focus helps students know what really matters right now.

10. Student Bulletin Board That Doubles as a Memory Book   Another way I simplified my wall space and saved my sanity at the end of the year was by creating a Memory Book bulletin board (see Figures 7.2–7.8). Teachers inside The Organized Teacher Club are doing the same thing. Instead of waiting until May to scramble through piles of student work and fight over the binding machine, they set up the memory books throughout the year as a living display. Each student has a file folder with prongs, hung low under the whiteboard where they can easily add to it. Anytime they finish a seasonal writing activity, directed drawing, or reflection piece that has two holes already punched at the top of the paper, they know to hang it on their folder when complete. The wall itself becomes a rotating display of student work, but the best part is that by June, the memory books are already finished, which means no late-night laminating or frantic binding required. At the end of the year, the folders come down and go home as a keepsake. Students love flipping through their work and laughing at their "first day of school portraits," and teachers love knowing that they've created both a functional display and a treasured yearbook without the stress.

How to Set Up a Memory Book Bulletin Board

1. Gather materials.

   - File folders with prongs

   - Two-hole punch

   - Seasonal writing/art activities

2. Create bulletin board.

   - Cut the file folder in half so that one file folder can be used for two students (see Figure 7.2).

      - Hang file folders low enough so students can reach them independently.

      - Staple each folder onto the wall in a straight line. Staple each corner and the middle of the folder (see Figure 7.3).

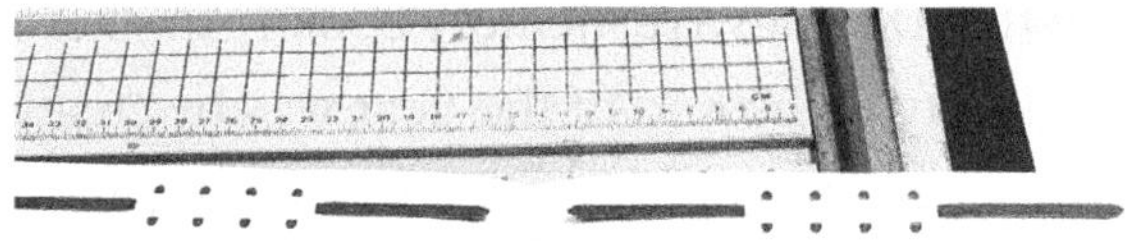

Figure 7.2   Cut file folders in half for memory book bulletin board

Figure 7.3 Staple file folders onto the wall

- Place a number die cut next to the folder so you can easily reuse this bulletin board again next year if you number your students (see Figure 7.4). If you want to personalize it, you can have students write their name on an index card staple it next to the number. You can also do the same with their photo.

3. Prepare student work.

- Copy the activity that will be hung onto the memory book onto white copy paper, cardstock, or bright paper.

- Take the entire class set of copies and double hole punch it before passing out (see Figure 7.5).

- Train students: if they see hole punches at the top of their paper, it goes straight onto their memory book when it's completed.

Figure 7.4 Place a number next to each folder to reuse each year
Courtesy of Easy Teaching Tools, LLC

Figure 7.5 Use a double hole punch before passing out student work

134

The Organized Teacher Toolkit

4. Rotate work throughout the year.

- Add monthly reflections, seasonal writing, or artwork (see Figures 7.6 and 7.7).
- Include photo collages for a yearbook feel.

5. Finish strong.

- Print memory book covers with student photos and class details.
- Let students add the covers themselves and flip through their "year in review."
- Have students gently pull their memory book off the wall at the end of the year, remove the staples, and take it home.

Tip: Keep one area of the wall just for these folders so you always have an up-to-date student work display *and* you never have to panic about end-of-year memory books again.

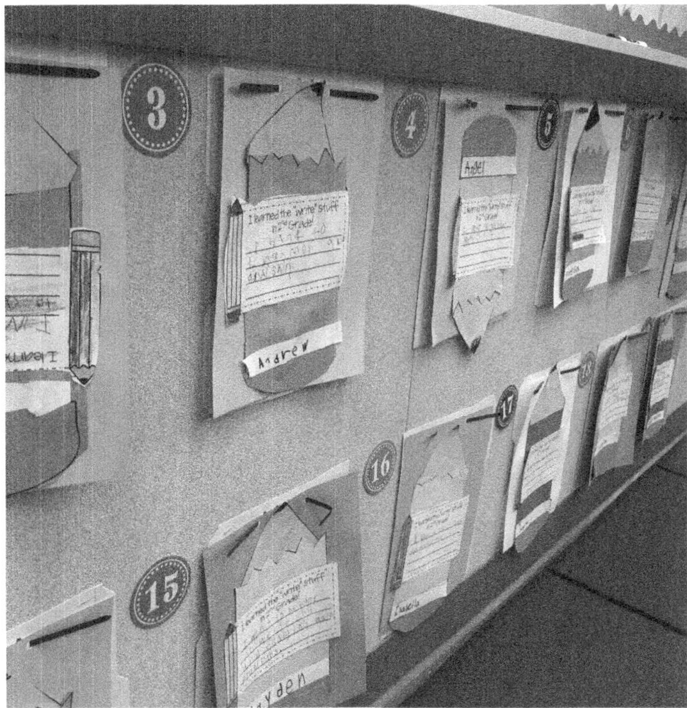

Figure 7.6   Student writing

Figure 7.7   Student self-portraits

Figure 7.8   Add a cover to memory books at the end of the year

Teachers especially love that this bulletin board makes it look like they always have it together. Because the memory books are updated monthly and sometimes even weekly, the display never feels stale. Administrators walking in see fresh student work, evidence of consistent writing and art projects, and a classroom environment that's clearly celebrating growth. It's one of those rare systems that checks all the boxes: it keeps your walls purposeful, impresses visitors, and actually saves you time in the long run.

Reflect and Reset

If you're not sure whether your walls are helping or hurting, step into your classroom as if you were a new student. What's the first thing your eye goes to? Is it clear where to find important references? Does the room feel calm and focused, or chaotic and busy? Better yet, ask your students what wall displays they actually use. You may be surprised by their honesty because often the charts we spend the most time perfecting are the ones they never look at.

Remember: Wall space is a tool, not a scrapbook. It should serve you and your students, not overwhelm you. The goal isn't to impress visitors with how much you can fit on your bulletin boards, it's to make sure that every item on your walls has a clear purpose and function.

Action Items for Wall Space

- Prioritize visibility: put anchor charts and references where students will actually use them.
- Start the year with mostly blank walls and build them together with student learning.
- Dedicate one bulletin board or section for student work and rotate it monthly.
- Stick to a simple color scheme or consistent borders to create cohesion.
- Post only what you've taught and trained students to use.
- Give yourself permission to take things down if they're not serving a purpose.

The Physical Classroom Environment

Wall Space Audit: Keep, Rotate, Remove

When your walls feel busy, it can be hard to know what to take down. Use this simple audit to decide what earns its place in your classroom:

Keep

Anchor charts you've explicitly taught and students actively use.

Word walls, math strategies, or reference tools that support current units.

Student work that reflects effort and builds classroom pride.

Calming or inspirational visuals that add warmth without distraction.

Rotate

Seasonal decorations or bulletin boards—refresh every month or quarter.

Student work displays—swap projects so every student gets represented.

Anchor charts—move older ones into a binder or chart stand for reference.

Inspirational quotes—keep one or two visible, store the rest to use later.

Remove

Outdated charts or posters from past units that students no longer need.

Visuals you put up because you "might" need them someday.

Decorations that compete for attention with instructional content.

Duplicates (e.g., two posters covering the same concept).

Of course, walls are only one part of your classroom environment. Just as important is what happens on the floor, the way you arrange desks, tables, and learning spaces. Layout determines how students interact, how easily you can move around, and whether your room feels chaotic or calm. Let's take a closer look at how classroom layout shapes learning.

Classroom Layout

Classroom layout is one of the most visible ways you communicate your teaching priorities to students. Rows of desks, for example, may emphasize individual focus and direct instruction, while clusters encourage collaboration and discussion. U-shaped or circle arrangements can foster inclusion, giving every student a clear line of sight to both the teacher and their peers. Research from the HEAD Project mentioned earlier highlights layout as a key factor influencing student progress, showing that when space is flexible and aligned to instructional goals, students demonstrate higher levels of engagement. The physical arrangement of desks, tables, and learning zones tells students what kinds of interactions are valued and can either encourage or discourage participation.

Rows   Rows are one of the most traditional layouts, often associated with testing or lecture-based instruction. They minimize distractions and make it easy for students to focus on the teacher or board at the front of the room. However, rows can limit collaboration and may leave quieter students less engaged. Rows are best used when you want to maximize attention on direct instruction or assessments.

Table Groups (Clusters)   This is what I used most of the time with my students. Clusters of desks or tables encourage collaboration and peer learning. They're ideal for project-based work, cooperative learning, and small-group discussions. The downside is that some students may get off-task more easily, and it can be harder for the teacher to have all students' attention at once. One way around this that worked well for me was rather than having all four desks facing each other, you can have two desks side-by-side and the other two desks facing forward. Clusters work well when the learning objective is social, interactive, or hands-on.

U-Shaped   A U-shaped layout provides every student with a clear view of the teacher and their peers. It supports whole-class discussions, Socratic seminars, and lessons where interaction is key. The open center space can also be used for demonstrations or student presentations. On the downside, U-shapes take up a lot of space and may not work well in smaller classrooms.

The Physical Classroom Environment

Circle or Horseshoe Similar to a U-shape but more enclosed, circles create a strong sense of community and equality in the classroom. This arrangement removes the "front of the room," signaling that everyone's contributions are valued. Circles are best for discussion-heavy lessons or restorative circles but may not be practical for every subject or activity.

Flexible Seating Flexible seating is a growing trend where students choose from a variety of seating options like beanbags, stools, standing desks, floor cushions, or traditional chairs. But at the end of the day, the intention is to give students a choice on where to work. Research shows flexible seating can reduce anxiety and support focus, especially for students who need movement. The challenge is maintaining structure and ensuring students choose spots that support their learning. Clear expectations are key to making flexible seating successful. I have used flexible seating with my students and always encourage brand new teachers to hold off on implementing full-on flexible seating for a few years because it does bring its own set of challenges. If you want to start small, consider giving your students choice during independent reading or adding table risers for a standing table option. But no need to swap out all of your furniture just yet!

Hybrid Models Many teachers use a mix of these layouts. For example, you might keep a few rows for focused instruction, add clusters for group projects, and create a small reading corner with flexible seating. Hybrid models allow you to match the physical layout to the type of work students are doing, without committing to a single style.

The Organized Teacher Toolkit

Layout	Advantages	Challenges	Best Uses
Rows	• Minimizes distractions • Easy teacher oversight • Clear line of sight to front	• Limits collaboration • Passive learning environment	Direct instruction, tests, focused writing, lectures
Table Groups	• Encourages collaboration • Supports group projects • Builds peer learning	• Can lead to off-task behavior • Harder for whole-class attention	Project-based learning, cooperative activities, centers
U-Shaped	• Every student faces teacher and peers • Great for discussion • Open space for demos	• Takes up more space • Hard to fit in small rooms	Class discussions, presentations, debates, Socratic seminars
Circle/ Horseshoe	• Creates community feel • Equal participation • Removes "front of room" dynamic	• Space intensive • Hard for writing-intensive tasks	Restorative circles, community-building, literature circles, open discussions
Flexible Seating	• Student choice reduces anxiety • Supports movement needs • Increases comfort	• Can feel chaotic without structure • Requires clear expectations	Independent reading, collaborative projects, classrooms with diverse needs
Hybrid Models	• Blends benefits of multiple layouts • Adapts to different activities • Flexible use of space	• Requires planning and rearranging • May confuse routines if not managed	Teachers who mix direct instruction, group work, and independent learning

The Physical Classroom Environment

Remember, effective layouts don't have to be permanent. Many teachers rotate between configurations throughout the year, or even the day, depending on the lesson. It's ok to mix things up or change things that aren't working. I can't tell you how many times I changed my room around at the beginning of the year because the configuration wasn't working or there was too much traffic in certain areas of the room.

When you look around your classroom right now, what is your layout communicating to your students about how you expect them to learn and interact, and is that the message you want to send?

You already know this but strategic use of space can also reduce behavioral challenges: placing students who need extra support near the front or creating "buffer zones" between particularly chatty groups helps maintain focus. Adding clear pathways for movement minimizes distractions and makes it easier for you to circulate around the room. Ultimately, the best classroom layouts are intentional, flexible, and responsive, changing as your students' needs and your instructional goals evolve. Designing the physical environment of your classroom is about more than colors, lighting, or where the desks go. It's about creating a space that reflects your values, supports your students, and makes daily teaching feel lighter instead of heavier. The research is clear: when the environment is intentional, students thrive. But research alone won't change your classroom, you will. Now that you've got the big-picture principles in mind, it's time to get practical and start thinking about how your classroom actually *flows* from day to day.

The next step is to consider how different areas of your classroom function because creating clear zones for learning activities can be just as powerful as where students sit.

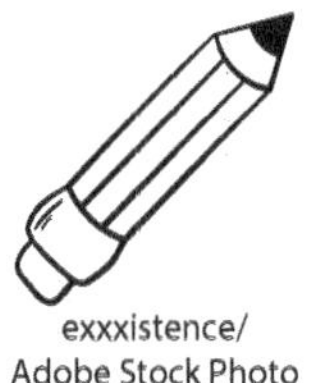

Task: What two ideas from this chapter are you going to implement in your classroom right now?

exxxistence/
Adobe Stock Photo

Chapter 8

Classroom Layout

Classroom Flow

Think about how you feel when you walk into a cluttered grocery store where aisles are blocked and signs are unclear. It's stressful, right? You waste time trying to figure out where to go and bump into other people along the way. Now, compare that to a well-organized store with wide aisles, clear signage, and logical placement. The second space feels easier, calmer, and more inviting.

Your classroom is no different. When your physical space "flows," students know where to be, how to move, and what to do without constant reminders from you. A well-designed classroom doesn't just look nice, it reduces behavior challenges, saves instructional time, and makes your life easier. In this section, we'll break down three key areas of classroom flow: high traffic areas, zones, and proximity/visibility. Then we'll walk through practical steps for getting started so you can set up a space that works for both you and your students.

High Traffic Areas

High traffic areas are those spots where students naturally gather and move frequently like doorways, supply stations, cubbies or backpack hooks, the pencil sharpener, and the line-up area. If these areas aren't set up thoughtfully, you'll find yourself dealing with bottlenecks, pushing, and wasted time every day.

Do you have any areas like that in your room?

Why it matters:

- Congested traffic areas create friction, both literally and figuratively. Students bump into each other, which can quickly escalate into arguments or off-task behavior.

- Wasted transition time adds up. If every line-up or supply grab takes an extra two minutes, you've lost hours of instructional time by the end of the month.

- Clear pathways promote safety, especially in emergencies when you need students to exit quickly and calmly.

Action Items for high traffic areas:

- Keep doorways clear: Avoid placing bookshelves, teacher desks, or supply carts directly near the classroom entrance. Students need space to enter and exit without crowding.

- Create flow "lanes": Use rugs, tape, sit spots, or furniture placement to suggest clear walking paths to common destinations.

- Separate major stations: Don't put the pencil sharpener, supply shelves, and turn-in bins in the same corner. Spread them out to reduce clumping.

- Designate waiting spots: For things like the pencil sharpener, mark a spot on the floor where students wait their turn, so the area stays orderly.

- Anticipate transitions: Think about the busiest moments such as arrival, center rotations, and dismissal. Do students have enough space to move without tripping over backpacks or crowding each other?

During your busiest transition times—arrival, lining up, or rotating through centers—where do students get stuck or crowded in your classroom? What's one adjustment you could make to open up the flow?

Once you've cleared the pathways and reduced bottlenecks in your high traffic areas, the next step is to think about how the rest of your space functions, by creating intentional zones that guide students' behavior and make your classroom run more smoothly.

Classroom Zones

Zones are the backbone of an organized classroom. Classroom zones are like invisible signposts that tell students what kind of work happens in each space. When your room is divided into clear, purposeful areas such as a reading corner, small-group table, supply station, or independent work zone allows students to move more confidently and independently because they know exactly what's expected in each area. Zones reduce the constant stream of "Where do I go?" or "What do I do next?" questions, freeing up your mental energy to focus on teaching. They also help maintain order and flow; instead of every student rushing to the same place at once, traffic spreads out naturally. In short, thoughtful zoning makes your classroom more self-sufficient and efficient. I'm sharing several classroom zones that teachers use in their classroom that may be helpful for you as you create zones or reflect on the zones you already have in place.

Whole Group Instruction Zone

This is where your class gathers for direct teaching, read-alouds, or discussions. It might be the carpet area in an elementary classroom or desks arranged in rows or a U-shape in upper grades.

Action Items:

- Make sure every student has a clear line of sight to you and the board.

- Keep distractions (like supply bins) out of this area.

- Use a rug, tape, or arrangement of furniture to define the space clearly. A large rug with clear boundaries works well to keep students organized in their individual spot (see Figure 8.1).

- To cut down on transition time, consider having your students sit in number-order during direct instruction and let them sit in any spot during read-aloud time to be more flexible.

Figure 8.1 Organized rug area for whole group instruction
Courtesy of Easy Teaching Tools, LLC

Small-Group Instruction Zone

A teacher table or small group reading corner where you can work with a handful of students at a time is absolutely necessary. It's also a great place to have students work who need a quieter space away from other students to focus (see Figure 8.2).

Action Items:

- Keep it close to your supplies (leveled readers, manipulatives, intervention tools) but positioned so you can still see the rest of the room.

- Keep a supply caddy on the table so students don't have to bring materials with them so you can get started quickly.

Figure 8.2 Small group table

Independent Time Zone

Students need a spot for quiet, focused work. This can be their desk, a table, or even a designated corner or area (see Figure 8.3).

Action Items:

- Reduce visual clutter in this zone to help with focus.
- Provide options for students who work better standing, at a table, or sitting on the floor with a clipboard.
- Keep supplies for independent work (pencils, paper) within easy reach so students don't need to get up often.

Early Finisher Zone

What happens when students finish before others? Having a clear zone prevents them from disrupting classmates.

Figure 8.3   A student using a lap desk to work independently

Action Items:

- Stock this area with fast-finisher activities like puzzles, task cards, or books (see Figure 8.4).

- Keep expectations consistent: this is a quiet zone, not free time for chatting.

- Rotate materials periodically to keep interest high.

Centers Zone

Centers are the heart of active, hands-on learning in many classrooms. They work best when students know exactly where to go. I always had a table leader who would be in charge of picking up center materials and bringing them back to the group so that the area wouldn't get crowded (see Figure 8.5). Each group would work in a different place in the room.

The Organized Teacher Toolkit

Figure 8.4 The math activities students choose when finished early

Figure 8.5 Center materials up close

Figure 8.6 Center materials stations

Action Items:

- Clearly label each center with a sign or symbol so students can find it independently.
- Space centers apart to reduce noise and crowding.
- Provide all necessary materials at each station to cut down on unnecessary movement (see Figure 8.6).

Technology Zone

Computers, tablets, or listening stations need their own space.

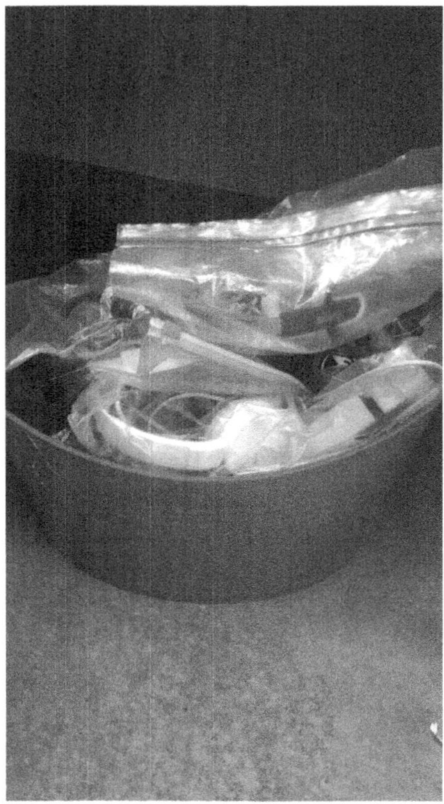

Figure 8.7   Individual headphone storage in a Ziploc bag

Action Items:

- Keep chargers, headphones, and devices organized with bins or labeled shelves (see Figures 8.7 and 8.8).

- Post simple troubleshooting steps so students can handle minor tech issues without always asking you (see Figure 8.9). Consider assigning two technology helpers who can also help while you're running small groups.

- Position this zone where you can easily see screens for monitoring (see Figure 8.10).

- If you don't have great storage, consider using letter trays and zip tie them together to store Chromebooks or iPads (see Figure 8.11).

Figure 8.8 Numbered Chromebooks for easy retrieval and return

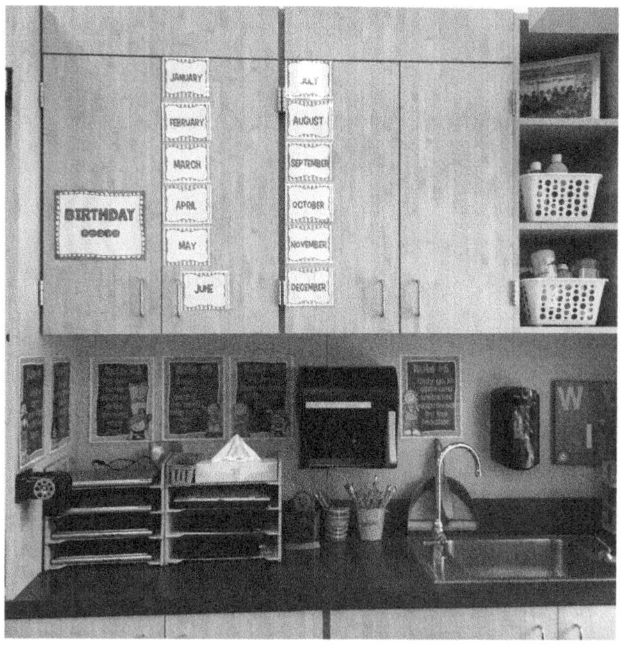

Figure 8.9 Technology rules posted

Figure 8.10 Desktop computers that can be seen when running small groups

Figure 8.11 Letter trays being used as technology storage

Library Zone

Your classroom library should invite students in and make reading feel special. I loved creating a space that my students wanted to spend time in so I made sure it was cozy and welcoming. It evolved over the years and what I ended up with was functional and also doubles as our class meeting-place oftentimes as students loved sitting on the benches and stools (see Figures 8.12 and 8.13).

Action Items:

- Organize books by category and label bins clearly (see Figure 8.14).
- Use comfortable seating like pillows, beanbags, or small chairs to make it cozy (see Figure 8.15).

Figure 8.12 Our inviting classroom library

Figure 8.13 Stools students sat on

Figure 8.14 Labeled book bins

Figure 8.15 Comfortable seating and pillows

- Consider adding soft lighting to make it extra comfortable and inviting.
- Keep the library separate from noisy or high-traffic areas.

Supplies Zone

A central supply station keeps materials accessible without constant interruptions. This is a great place for students to grab supplies when theirs run out (see Figure 8.16). Ensure that students tell you when they grab the last supply so that you can replace it.

Figure 8.16 Common supplies students ran out of

Action Items:

- Use labeled bins for common supplies (scissors, glue, markers).
- Teach students to take *one* item at a time and either return it neatly or keep it at their desk.
- Place the supply station in a spot that doesn't block key pathways.

Turn-In Work Zone

Students need one clear spot for finished work. This will eliminate asking where to turn in work and it will also cut down on missing papers. I'll share exactly how to set this up in Chapter 11.

Action Items:

- Use a single tray, bin, or file sorter.

- Label bins by subject if needed, but keep the system simple.

- Place it near your desk or on top of your student cubbies for easy collection but not where students will crowd during transitions.

Backpack/Personal Item Zone

Backpacks and jackets can cause chaos if not contained. The set up of this zone will also depend on the weather where you live.

Action Items:

- Use hooks, cubbies, or a designated wall area.

- Numbering the hooks and cubbies make it easy for students to hang up supplies quickly and easily.

- Keep this zone near the door to reduce congestion during arrival and dismissal.

- Establish routines for how and when students can access their backpacks during the day.

Calm-Down or Self-Regulation Zone

A quiet space where students can reset emotions without disrupting class.

Action Items:

- Stock it with a sand timer, stress balls, fidgets, coloring pages, or reflection sheets. Teach routines so it's a supportive, not punitive, space.

- If you can, include a comfortable seat or chair for one student to visit at a time.

Collaboration Zone

A designated area for group projects or brainstorming. I know this isn't always realistic so during these projects, we would simply spread out around the room.

Action Items:

- Provide a large table, whiteboard or chart paper, or floor space for students to spread out and work together.

Presentation Zone

An area for student speeches, read-alouds, or performances.

Action Items:

- Leave a bit of open floor near your whole-group area or the board where students can stand comfortably to present.

Anchor Chart/Reference Wall Zone

A wall or bulletin board devoted to key content (vocabulary walls, math strategies, anchor charts).

Action Items:

- Place it where students can easily see it from their seats; keep it updated and uncluttered.
- Consider putting phonics patterns or other key concepts on 18×24 construction paper, hole punch the corner, and add to a binder ring. Place that collection of charts on a push pin low enough on the wall for students to easily take off and access it when needed.
- You can also use a heavy duty magnetic curtain rod to display anchor charts that were made with students, otherwise it's a poster (see Figures 8.17 and 8.18).

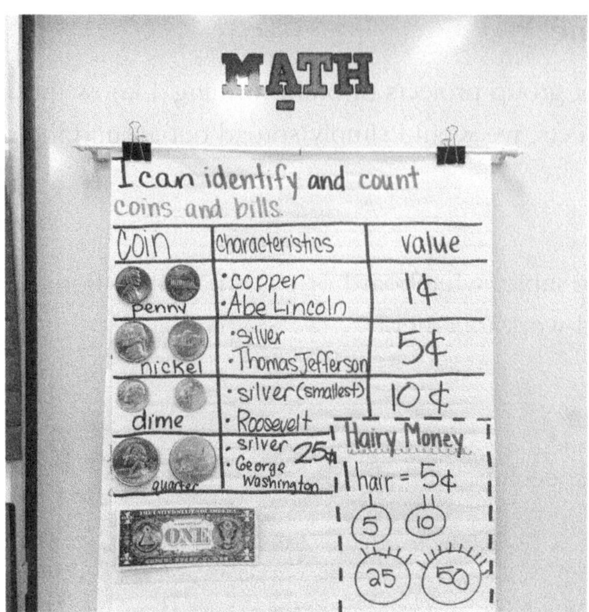

Figure 8.17 Magnetic curtain rod

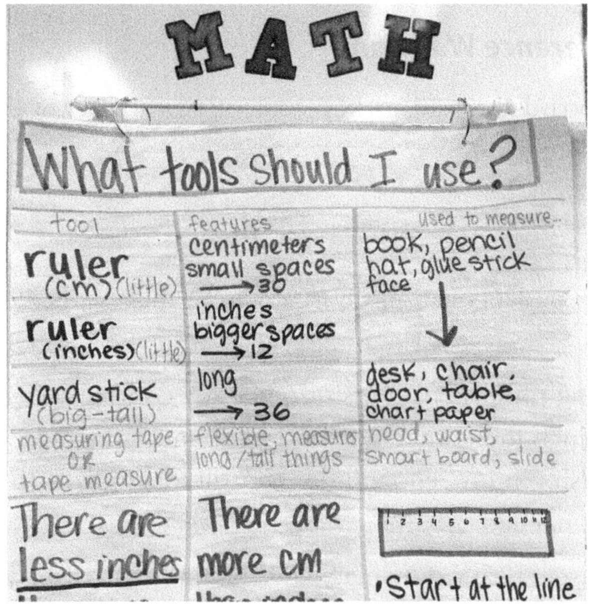

Figure 8.18 Binder rings being used to attach multiple anchor charts students can flip through

The Organized Teacher Toolkit

Student Work Display Zone

A space that creates community, celebrates student success, and builds pride.

Action Items:

- Rotate work often so every student sees their contributions highlighted.
- This can even be a small bulletin board near the drinking fountain where students can bring in a postcard from a trip, a recently earned medal from soccer to be displayed, or a family photo to showcase for a limited time and then will be sent home. It's a great way to share a bit about what's happening in their life throughout the year.

Teacher Work Zone

Even if you don't have a big desk, you need a small, organized space for your own materials.

Action Items:

- Keep it streamlined and functional, just what you need daily, so it doesn't become a clutter magnet.

The beauty of classroom zones is that they give both you and your students a sense of calm and clarity. When every space has a purpose, you spend less energy directing traffic and more time actually teaching. But remember, zones don't have to be perfect on the first try. They're meant to grow and shift with your students, just like your teaching does. So give yourself permission to experiment, to rearrange, and to let your classroom evolve because what worked with your students last year may not work with your students this year and that's okay.

Ask yourself: What kind of learning do I want to invite into this space, and how can the environment make that possible? When you approach your room with that mindset, you're not just setting up furniture, you're designing a learning experience.

Once your classroom zones are clearly defined, the next step is to think about how you position yourself and your students within those spaces because proximity and visibility are what allow you to truly manage the room and keep learning on track.

Proximity and Visibility

Proximity and visibility are the silent management tools built into your classroom design. The way desks, tables, and zones are arranged determines whether you can move easily between students, whether you can see every corner of the room, and whether students feel accountable for staying on task. When students know you can reach them in seconds or that you have a clear line of sight no matter where they sit they're far less likely to drift off or misbehave. At the same time, good visibility and access make it easier for you to provide help quickly, keep students safe, and use your energy on teaching rather than constant redirection.

I remember one year when I was implementing flexible seating, I set up an IKEA bookshelf to separate my library off from one part of my room but in doing that, I didn't have a clear view of my students at the standing table or computers. I knew this could be a problem but wanted to see what would happen anyways once I welcomed my new group of students. Within the first week of school, I moved that bookshelf to the other side of the library so I could have a clear view of all of the work areas in my classroom to ensure my students were on task and safe while I was working with small groups across the room.

The best classroom setups allow you to see and reach every student quickly. If you can't move easily between desks or if certain students are hidden from view, you'll spend more time managing behavior than teaching.

If you notice that behaviors tend to increase while students are working independently during centers and you're running small groups, I've got one of the very best tips for you that I learned early on in my career, and whenever I share it with teachers, they absolutely love it!

Did you know that you can easily redirect students from across the room without saying a word . . . using a laser pointer?

The Organized Teacher Toolkit

One of my favorite memories about the power of visibility happened while I was running a small reading group at my table. Across the room, I noticed a student at an independent center starting to drift, his group was working, but he was off task and staring into space. Instead of stopping my reading group or raising my voice, I quietly clicked on my laser pointer and placed the red dot right next to his hand on the desk. His eyes snapped back to me, then to his group's work, and he got right back on task. The rest of his group never even noticed, and my small group kept going without interruption. Later, we laughed about it, and it became a running class joke: "The laser sees all." It was a small moment, but a powerful reminder that visibility doesn't just keep students accountable, it allows you to manage behavior with humor and subtlety, all while staying focused on the students in front of you. When students know you can see them no matter where you are in the room, they're much more likely to stay engaged and on task.

Why It Matters:

- Easy access reduces misbehavior and students are less likely to go off-task when they know you can be beside them in seconds.

- Visibility supports safety in case of emergencies.

- Being able to circulate naturally also lets you provide more individual feedback.

Action Items for Proximity and Visibility:

- Arrange desks or tables so you can walk the room in a full circle without obstacles.

- Avoid "dead zones" where students can't be seen.

- Keep your small-group table positioned so you still have a line of sight across the room.

- Make sure high-need students (behavioral, medical, or academic) are seated where you can reach them quickly.

- Get yourself a laser pointer to use to silently redirect students!

Proximity and visibility may not seem as exciting as a new set of centers or a cozy classroom library, but they are the quiet anchors that make everything else work. When

As you begin to design your classroom layout or look around your classroom, are there any spots where students can disappear from your view or where it's hard for you to move quickly? What small adjustment could you make this week to improve your proximity and visibility?

you can move easily around the room and see every student, you send a powerful message: *I'm present, I'm available, and I care about what you're doing.* That presence builds accountability, but it also builds trust. Students know they can't slip through the cracks, and they also know you'll be there when they need support. The best part is, you don't need elaborate systems, just intentional design and the willingness to adjust when something isn't working. A classroom where you can see and reach every learner is a classroom where students feel both safe and seen, and that is the foundation of meaningful learning.

Now that we've looked at how to manage high-traffic areas, create purposeful zones, and design for proximity and visibility, it's time to put it all together and start mapping out your own classroom space.

How to Get Started

Designing your classroom can feel overwhelming at first, especially when you're staring at a room full of desks, shelves, and supplies with no clear plan. The good news is, you don't have to figure it all out in one sitting, and you definitely don't need to get it perfect on the first try. Think of your classroom setup as a work in progress, something you sketch, test, and adjust until it feels right for you and your students. The goal isn't to create a Pinterest-perfect space, but a functional environment that makes teaching easier and learning smoother.

For teachers who are brand new to a space, a step-by-step approach is helpful:

Step 1: Sketch Your Floor Plan

Draw a quick map of your classroom and mark major features: doors, windows, outlets, and built-ins. This helps you visualize options without moving heavy furniture.

The Organized Teacher Toolkit

Step 2: Identify Zones First or Place Desks First

Zones First Approach: Decide where your library, supplies, centers, and whole-group space will go. Then fit desks and tables around those zones.

- *Pros:* Prioritizes function; ensures activity areas have the space they need.
- *Cons:* Desk placement might feel like an afterthought.

Desks First Approach: Arrange student seating first, then fit zones into remaining areas.

- *Pros:* Guarantees every student has a comfortable seat.
- *Cons:* Zones may feel cramped or awkward.

There's no right or wrong approach—it depends on your teaching style and priorities.

Step 3: Test and Tweak

Live with your setup for a week, then ask: Is traffic flowing smoothly? Are students clear on where to go? Can I reach everyone easily?

Most importantly: It's absolutely okay to move your room around if it's not working. Too often we think we have to "get it perfect" during setup week. The truth is, your classroom should evolve with your students. If a new seating chart or zone arrangement will make life easier, make the change! Flexibility is part of good classroom management.

But what if you've already been teaching for years, or your room feels full to the brim? You don't have to start over. Sometimes the most powerful changes are the smallest ones: shifting a supply station to reduce bottlenecks, moving one table to open up a pathway, or rethinking how students turn in work. Veteran teachers often find that tweaking just one or two areas completely transforms the flow of the room.

Quick Wins for Established Classrooms:

- Move your turn-in bin closer to the door to cut down on transition chaos.
- Clear one pathway so you can make a full loop around the room without obstacles.

- Shift your small-group table to a spot with better visibility.

- Relocate backpacks or personal items to reduce tripping hazards.

- Create a micro "quiet zone" with one chair and a basket of books for students who need a reset.

- Audit your supplies and ask yourself if there are stations students rarely use? If so, simplify and reclaim the space.

What's one small change you could make in your classroom this week—whether it's moving a bin, shifting a table, or opening up a pathway—that would make the flow easier for you and your students?

Whether you're brand new or a seasoned veteran, the mindset is the same: your classroom setup should serve *you and your students*. Start with one intentional change, observe the difference, and let your room evolve over time so you can have results like Lydia.

Real Teacher Talk

I feel like my classroom flows now. I'm not running around thinking on my feet for every decisions. I have a plan and a purpose for each instruction because my classroom is organized. My students are able to have more time to work and learn without waiting for me to decide. —Lydia B.

Once your classroom space is set up to support learning, the next step is organizing the work that happens inside it. A well-designed room creates the foundation, but it's your planning systems that keep everything running smoothly day after day. In the next chapter, we'll dig into practical organization strategies for lesson planning so you spend less time scrambling and more time teaching with confidence.

exxxistence/
Adobe Stock Photo

Task: Sketch out your classroom layout using what you've learned from this chapter.

Chapter 9

Organization Systems to Save Time Lesson Planning

If you've ever sat down to plan lessons and ended up staring at a blinking cursor, scrolling Teachers Pay Teachers for "just the right" activity, or falling into a YouTube rabbit hole, you're not alone. Lesson planning can feel like one of the most never-ending parts of teaching because there's *always* another day, another standard, another activity to prep. And if we're being honest, it's also one of the easiest places to lose hours without realizing it.

A few years ago, I worked with a third-grade teacher named Melissa who told me she "basically lived at school" because of lesson planning. She'd stay until 6:00 most nights, dragging home stacks of materials, and still feel unprepared for the next day. When I asked her what was taking the most time, she admitted it wasn't just the planning itself, it was all the stuff around it. She'd sit down to plan math, get distracted by a new idea for her bulletin board, realize she needed to find a missing file, and then spend 30 minutes digging through her Google Drive. By the time she got back to planning, she was exhausted, frustrated, and already behind. Once Melissa learned how to set a clear planning rhythm and use batching strategies, she went from staying until dinner to leaving school at 4:15 most days with her lessons prepped for the entire week. The difference wasn't that she became more disciplined or "worked harder." The difference was that she had a system.

Here's the good news: planning doesn't have to take over your nights, weekends, and sanity like it did with Melissa. With the right systems, you can create lessons that are intentional, aligned, and engaging without spending endless hours on them. This chapter is about making lesson planning *work for you*, instead of feeling like you're constantly working for it.

I'll walk you through how to streamline your planning process so you spend less time hunting for resources and more time actually teaching them. You'll learn how to set yourself up for success with a monthly and weekly planning rhythm, batch similar tasks, and cut down on decision fatigue so you're not starting from scratch every single week.

By the time you finish this chapter, you'll have a system that allows you to walk into your classroom fully prepared—without sacrificing your evenings or Sunday afternoons. Because planning should support your teaching, not take over your life.

Backwards Planning to Cut Down Your Planning Time

If you've never backwards planned before, you're about to discover one of the biggest time-saving tools from The Organized Teacher System. Most teachers are told to "start with the standard," but in practice, that often gets lost when you're just trying to survive the week. Backwards planning is like giving your future self a giant gift because you do the heavy lifting up front so that planning later in the year takes a fraction of the time. Backwards planning is a simple reset: instead of starting with activities, you start with the end in mind. Instead of scrambling each Sunday night or spending your prep period staring at a blank lesson plan, you'll already know exactly what's coming, and you can plug activities straight into your plan book without reinventing the wheel.

Inside The Organized Teacher Club, I walk teachers through my full Organized Teacher System, where I show exactly how I backwards planned my entire school year.

One of our members, Tomeka, told me she no longer dreads planning because this process cut her planning time in half. "It's like I already did the hard work months ago," she said. "Now, I just pull from my map and I'm done."

Here's how you can use this system in your own classroom:

1. Gather Your Tools

   You'll need your pacing guides, your state or district standards, and a few writing utensils. If you have a printed or digital planning template, either the one I provide inside The Organized Teacher Club or the one in your plan book, keep that handy.

2. Map Out the Non-Negotiables

   Start by filling in the "big rocks" on your calendar, things like district benchmark testing dates, assessment windows, school breaks, conferences, and special events. These are your immovable pieces that everything else will work around.

3. Plan One Subject at a Time

   I recommend starting with math, since it tends to be the most straightforward. Look at your curriculum or standards and assign each unit to a specific month. Color-coding helps here, maybe red for math, blue for ELA, green for science. If your first math unit in August is Graphing, write "Graphing" in red under August. If September is Addition, add that next. Then move on to ELA, science, social studies, and any other core subjects you teach.

   To be able to fit in Science and Social Studies, I alternated between the two each month depending on our ELA unit and used a cross-curricular approach so that I could tie in content seamlessly.

   By the time you've done this for each subject, you'll have a year-long curriculum map that's easy to reference. This is your bird's-eye view or the "Year at a Glance" of your year (see Figures 9.1 and 9.2). You can use a digital or hard copy version.

Organization Systems to Save Time Lesson Planning

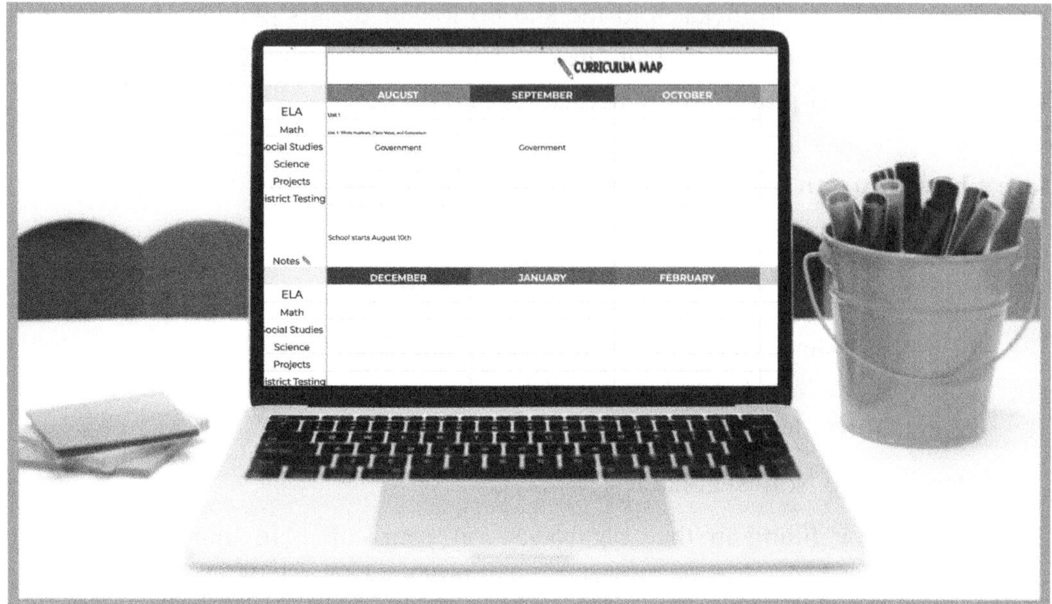

Figure 9.1   Digital curriculum map from The Organized Teacher Club

Scan to get this download

4. Monthly Prep Sessions

Here's where the magic happens. Once a month, choose a day to stay later than usual. Pull out your curriculum map, look ahead to the coming month, and gather all the resources, activities, and materials you'll need for those units. For me, I just grabbed all of my files, went through each one and grabbed what I thought I wanted to use and stacked those into a pile and put the stacked files aside.

You could put the activities in a designated "Upcoming Month" folder whether it's physical or digital, if you'd like but I put them in my "Copy" drawer from my three-drawer system to copy later. I'll share about this system soon!

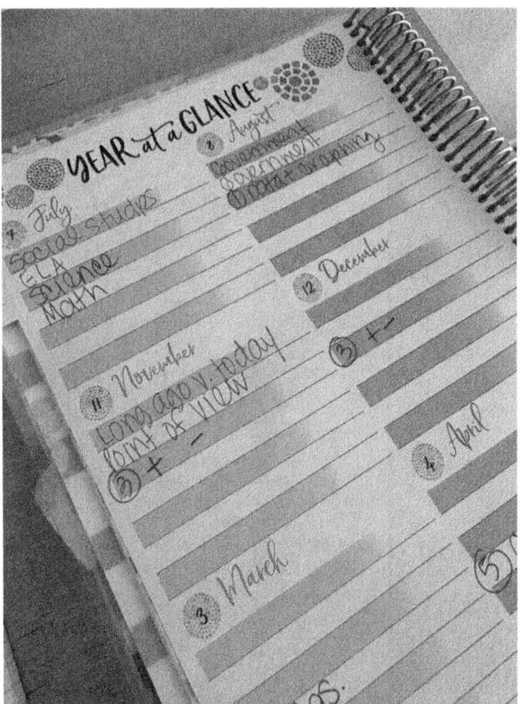

Figure 9.2 Year at a glance using the Teaching Texan Planner

5. Weekly Planning Made Simple

When it's time to plan each week, all you have to do is grab your "Upcoming Month" folder and plug activities into your lesson plans (see Figure 9.3). The decision-making has already been done, so you're not staring at a blank plan book wondering where to start—especially on days when you're tired or mentally maxed out.

Backwards planning works because it honors both your time and your boundaries. You're making decisions in advance, on your terms, instead of rushing to meet deadlines at the moment. And the best part? Every month, you'll thank yourself for putting in that work upfront.

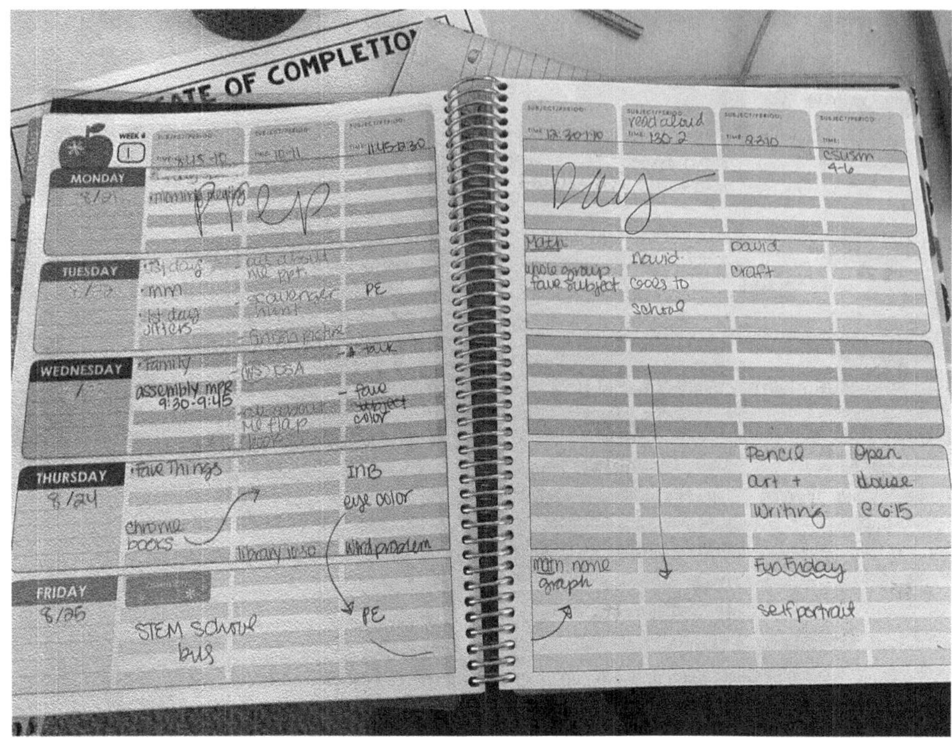

Figure 9.3   Lesson Plans for the week

Real Teacher Talk

The Organized Teacher System has helped me get better organized in activities, planning is easier, provided activities for centers and small groups, encouragement when I needed, and I got to go home earlier. —Caroldyne S.

Create a Planning Routine

If you've ever felt like lesson planning spills into every evening and weekend, it's usually because there's no clear end point and you're always chasing "just one more thing." That's why I love setting a routine where everything is planned, copied, and prepped

The Organized Teacher Toolkit

by Thursday, with Friday reserved only for organizing materials and swapping out centers. This system gives you a finish line every week, so you can walk out on Friday knowing your classroom (and your brain) are ready for Monday without the Sunday-night panic.

Planning by subject and batching makes the most sense because it keeps your brain focused in one lane, saves you from constantly switching gears, and allows you to go deeper and finish faster without the scattered feeling of juggling every subject at once. Here's a sample weekly planning schedule (see Figure 9.4) you can use to guide you and create your own. And to save you even more time, download the auto-populating Weekly To-Do List that allows you to input the daily planning task you're working on and it will autofill onto the to-do list so you aren't having to write the same thing week-after-week (see Figure 9.5).

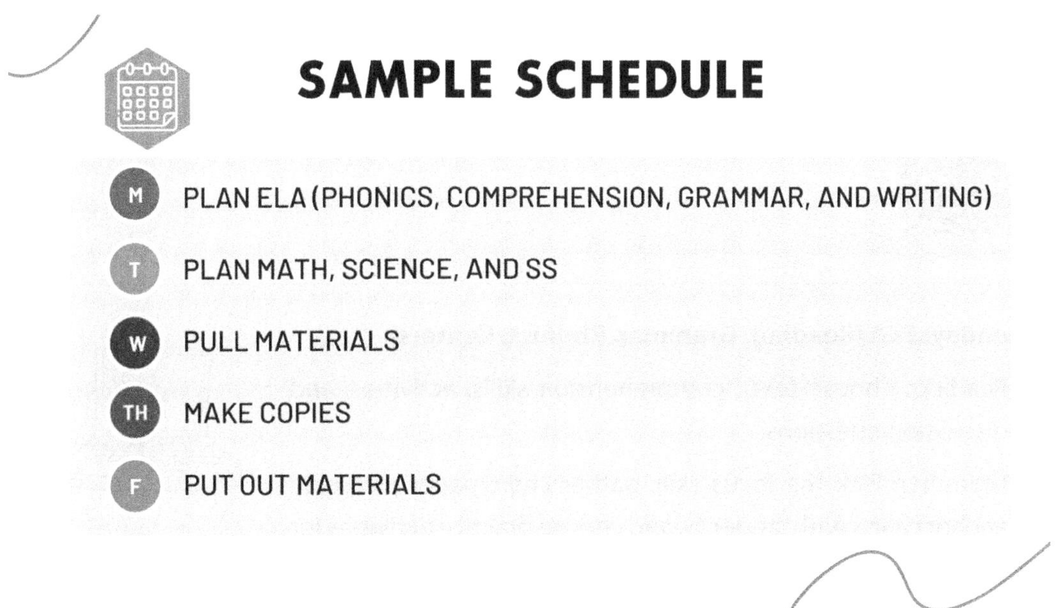

Figure 9.4   A weekly planning schedule you can make your own

Organization Systems to Save Time Lesson Planning

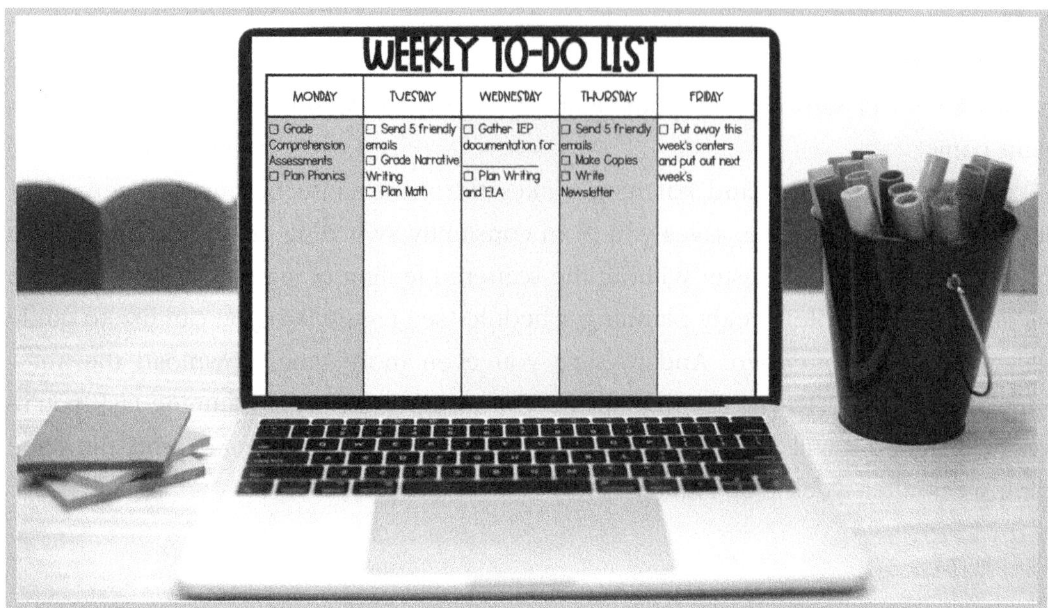

Figure 9.5 An auto-populating weekly schedule to help you complete your planning tasks

Scan to get this download

Monday: ELA (Reading, Grammar, Phonics, Centers)

- Reading: Choose texts, comprehension skills, activities, and discussion questions.

- Grammar: Pick the focus skill, gather chart paper to create anchor charts with students, and choose practice activities for independent practice and centers.

- Phonics/Spelling: Look at phonics patterns and plan word work activities for independent work and centers.

- Centers: Decide which activities students will work on that is a spiral review. Consider activities for a listening center, word work, grammar, comprehension, writing, and thematic work based on the season.

Tuesday: Math

- Outline lessons for each day (warm-up, model, practice, exit ticket).
- Plan small-group instruction or intervention.
- Select manipulatives, task cards, or digital practice.

Wednesday: Science/Social Studies and Copies

- Choose focus standard/unit topic. As I shared in the Backwards Planning section, one month I focused on Science and then next month I focused on Social Studies based on our ELA curriculum to tie it all in together and ensure I was able to teach as many standards as possible seamlessly. Use your best judgment and do what works best for you!
- Map out labs, projects, or readings.
- Prep graphic organizers, slides, or experiment supplies.
- Start making copies for everything planned for the upcoming week so far (ELA, Math, Science, Social Studies). If you are able to enlist help from an adult volunteer, consider having them make weekly copies for you.

Thursday: Writing and Copies Wrap-Up

- Plan mini-lessons, prompts, mentor texts, and conferencing goals.
- Finish all remaining copies for next week.
- Double-check the calendar (assemblies, holidays, assessments).

Friday: Materials & Centers

- Organize copies into a weekly copy tray for the upcoming week.
- Pull manipulatives, set up labs, prepare art project materials and anything else.
- Swap out centers for next week (Friday afternoon).

Organization Systems to Save Time Lesson Planning

Limit Distractions

Lesson planning eats time not just because it's hard, but because it's so easy to get pulled in a hundred directions. The biggest mistake teachers make when lesson planning is getting distracted and I promise that you're not alone. I'm going to show you

Can you start to see how this system will help you plan quickly?

five simple systems from The Organized Teacher System to manage and organize your lesson planning time so that you are focused and effective so that you can save time and cut your lesson planning time in half because a good, efficient teacher has a plan in place to make the best use of their time while still protecting it.

exxxistence/
Adobe Stock Photo

Now that you can see how this planning system can support you, create your own. Don't forget you can use the free Weekly Planning To-Do List included earlier in the chapter to support you.

Set a timer:

Remember the Time Timer from Chapter 4. This is a perfect time to use it. Give yourself a 45-minute block to plan one subject. The time limit keeps you moving instead of tinkering forever because done is better than perfect, right? Set a goal time to leave, lock your door, shut your blinds, put your phone on airplane mode, and respect the timer when it goes off.

Move away from your computer:

When you're planning, resist the urge to sit near your computer where you can be easily distracted. If you have to plan on your computer and you're tempted to open Pinterest, YouTube, or TPT, use the free Chrome extensions from Chapter 4 to keep you focused.

Create Copy Clips

If you use Post-its weekly to write down the same copy instructions, this is for you. Instead, get clothespins and write the number of copies on the bottom and the directions on the side of the clothespin. For example, it may say 24 and 1-1 which means 24 one-sided copies (see Figures 9.6 and 9.7). Clip your clothespins to the top of a small container or cup (see Figure 9.8). This is now where all of your planning materials will go so add whiteout tape, your favorite planning pens, highlighter, and any other tools you like to use. Keep this cup with your plan book so you're no longer wandering your room looking for your favorite planning pen again!

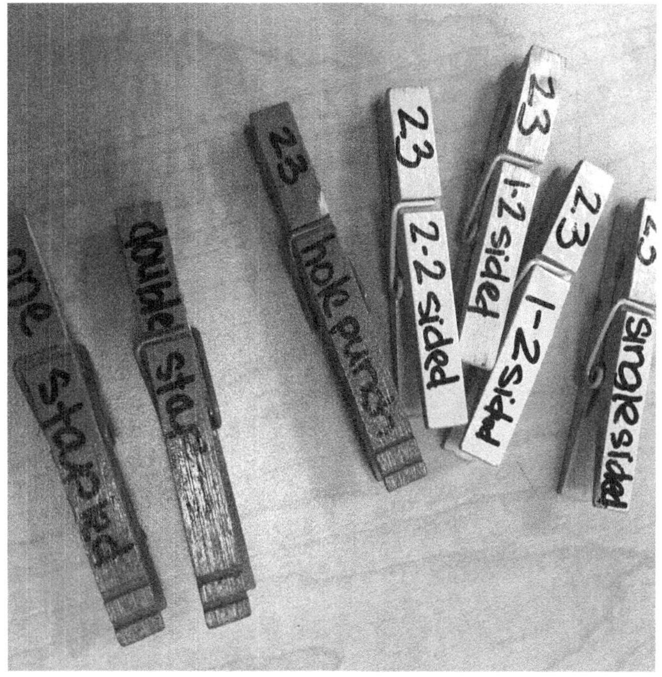

Figure 9.6 Copy clips with directions to save time

Organization Systems to Save Time Lesson Planning

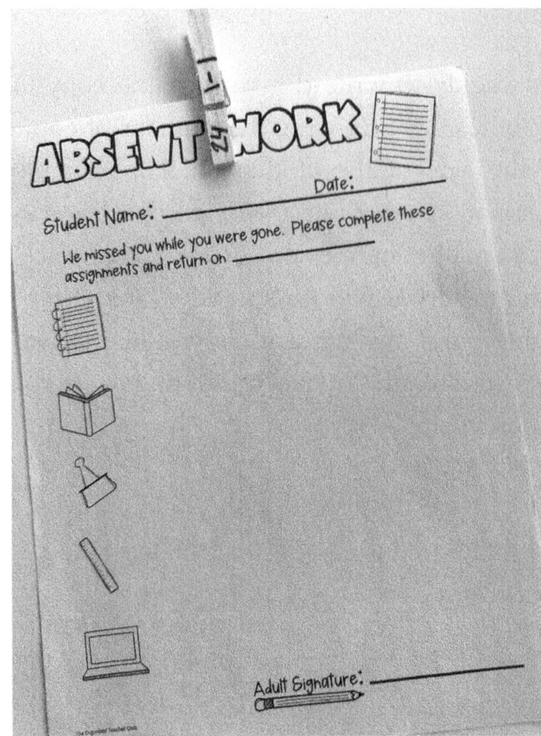

Figure 9.7   Copy clips can be easily attached to papers

Suggested Copy Clips Instructions

- 1-1 sided

- 1-2 sided

- 2-2 sided

- 2-1 sided

- Stapled

- Double stapled

- Laminated

When it comes to prepping your copies to be copied, as you're lesson planning, simply make a pile of the papers you want copied and use the correct copy clip to keep copies together. That's it! So you'll end up with a pile of 1-1 copies, 1-2 copies, 2-2 copies, and so-on. If you want something stapled, just clip that copy clip to the

The Organized Teacher Toolkit

Figure 9.8 A copy cup with planning utensils and copy clips

correct pile that needs to be stapled. Keep those copies in your "Copy" drawer of your three-drawer system until it's time to make copies.

If you have a copy person who volunteers and comes in to make your copies, simply leave your copies in your mailbox if it's in the same place as the copy machine and they can easily grab your originals and make copies. When they're done, they can leave all copies in your mailbox. Think of how much time this will save you instead of having to explain your directions every week!

This system works the same if you are the one who is making your copies. When your copies are made, simply take the clips off of your originals and place them back onto your copy cup to be used next week.

Place your original copies in your "File Me" drawer in your three-drawer organizer. If paperwork has been overwhelming, this will save you! Between copies, office memos, student work, and notes from caregivers, it's no wonder things end up stacked on every surface. That's why I created the three-drawer system, a simple way to give every paper a home so you can actually find what you need and it's one of the top-three favorite systems inside The Organized Teacher Club. All you need is a Sterilite three-drawer organizer in either a large or extra large. Historically, it's most cost-effective to purchase this at your favorite store rather than online (see Figure 9.9).

Organization Systems to Save Time Lesson Planning

Figure 9.9   Three-drawer system

Drawer 1: Grade Me

Student work waiting to be graded, all in one place.

Drawer 2: Copy Me

Papers you still need to run copies of (no more last-minute "Where did I put that?").

Drawer 3: File Me

Papers ready to be filed, passed back, or sent home in folders.

With labeled drawers, you'll never waste precious minutes hunting through stacks again. Everything has a home, and you can keep the flow of papers moving instead of piling up. These labels are editable so you can make it work for you, but these main drawers are the big areas that teachers typically struggle with.

The Organized Teacher Toolkit

Create a Paper Sorter for Your Weekly Plans

Once you've tamed the paper piles with the three-drawer system, the next step is to keep your copies organized. A simple paper sorter can completely change how prepared you feel each week. You can purchase one or create your own using leftover flat rate shipping boxes from the USPS in a size medium and hot-glue them together like I did in Figure 9.10.

On binder clips, label each tray with the day of the week. For the extra trays, label them "Next Week," "Following Week," and "Didn't Get To." If you're making your own paper sorter, use binder clips and label those!

Now, you can easily put your copies, posters, materials for your art project, and notes from the office that need to go home, in the correct tray. If you get ahead, you can put your copies in the "Next Week" or "Following Week" tray. When there's an unexpected fire drill or you simply run out of time for the day, you can take the activities you didn't get to and place them in the "Didn't Get To" tray and plug them into your plan book next week.

Figure 9.10   Paper sorter to store and organize copies for the week
Courtesy of Easy Teaching Tools, LLC

Organization Systems to Save Time Lesson Planning

Lesson planning will always be a part of teaching, it's not something you can skip. But it doesn't have to drain your evenings, weekends, and energy. When you batch by subject, set a clear weekly routine, and use simple systems like the three-drawer system and Copy Clips, you take back control of the process. Instead of scrambling to pull it all together at the last minute, you've got a rhythm that works for you every single week.

The real win here isn't just having neat drawers or trays full of copies. It's the peace of mind that comes from knowing you're ready. It's being able to leave school on Friday with your lessons and materials prepped, your centers swapped out, and your mind free to focus on your life outside of teaching because lesson planning should serve you, not the other way around.

What's one system or routine from this chapter that you can commit to trying this week to give yourself back more time and peace of mind?

With your lesson planning streamlined and your materials prepped ahead of time, you'll start to notice how much more space you have to focus on teaching. But planning is only half the battle, the other time-consuming piece is grading. Just like planning, grading can eat up evenings and weekends if there's no system in place. In the next chapter, we'll tackle grading time savers that will help you give meaningful feedback, stay on top of student work, and protect your personal time.

Task: Pick one system to set up and implement right now.

exxxistence/
Adobe Stock Photo

The Organized Teacher Toolkit

Chapter 10

Organization Systems to Save Time Grading

Idon't know about you, but grading always felt a lot like unloading the dishwasher for me. I hated doing it, but it had to be done. Because of that, piles of papers would stack up. They'd sit there taunting me, and I'd feel guilty the higher they grew. By the time I finally got around to grading the work, I was embarrassed to send it home weeks later. Can you relate?

Grading takes up so much of our time, and it's one of the biggest reasons teachers blur the boundary of leaving school work at school, because we drag stacks of papers home night after night. That's exactly why this chapter exists: to help you find practical grading systems that save time, reduce guilt, and give you your evenings and weekends back.

Recently, I asked teachers who've been leaving school before dark to share their favorite system from The Organized Teacher System that's made a massive difference in their teaching this year. The overwhelming majority said the grading system!

Real Teacher Talk

One teacher, Alyssa B., said, "I feel empowered with the tips and resources that have helped me to be more organized and efficient. For example, the class list helped me with my grading because I could grade tests and return them while keeping a copy of the scores. The class list helped me with keeping track of assignments, benchmarks, and absences."

We asked K–5 teachers inside The Organized Teacher Club the craziest place they've ever graded student work and this is what they said:

- In the bathroom, watching my younger daughter play in the tub. —Crystal G.

- Car dealership waiting for my car, hair salons, son's baseball game, on a plane, during school conventions, doctor's office while my son was getting his wisdom teeth pulled. —Leah C.

- In the car, at the beach, outside my backyard overlooking the garden, Panera Bread, at church (not the service, but during a special speaker talk), at a concert, or special ceremonies. You name it! I've done it! —Veronica P.

- In the hospital while awaiting my emergency procedure to be performed. —Jamie B.

- Doctor's office waiting room, in the car as my husband drove us out of state to celebrate our niece's baby dedication, in bed after an appendectomy. —Devin M.

- At a Major League Baseball game. Embarrassed my children to death! I still cheered at the proper time! No slacking on my part! —Beth H.

- At a bar celebrating a birthday, orchestra rehearsal, at the pool. My answers aren't too exciting. —Yoko T.

- On an airplane. And sitting on the floor in a hallway between rounds at my son's Lego Robotics tournament. —Leigh Ann S.

- In between performances at my daughters' show choir competitions. —Tracye H.

Do you have anything in common with these organized teachers? Where's the craziest place you've graded student work?

Grading List

One proven organization system that teachers need is a grading list. This allowed me to get work back a lot faster while doing it at school. All you need is your student work, a pen, and your grading checklist.

I used these grading lists daily for everything from tests, benchmarks, and absences to tracking returned assignments. They made it easy to grade quickly, keep accurate records, and get work back to students without weeks of delay. The simple act of checking off names kept me accountable and saved me from digging through piles of papers.

These lists auto-populate your student names to save time, which is why over 40,000 K–5 teachers are successfully using them throughout the day. I color-coded the lists for math, comprehension, grammar, phonics, and writing (see Figure 10.1). How would you color-code yours?

When students turned in an assessment to the turn-in basket, I'd paperclip the color-coded list to the top and place the assessments in my "Grade Me" drawer from my three-drawer system from Chapter 9. This kept all assessments together so I was no longer looking for misplaced tests and I could easily see whose tests were missing. When it came time to grade, I'd record the score on the grading list, and return the assessments back to my students, sometimes that same day. Since I already sent the assessments home, I could input the scores to our online gradebook later, which eliminated grading from piling up and students receiving feedback quickly.

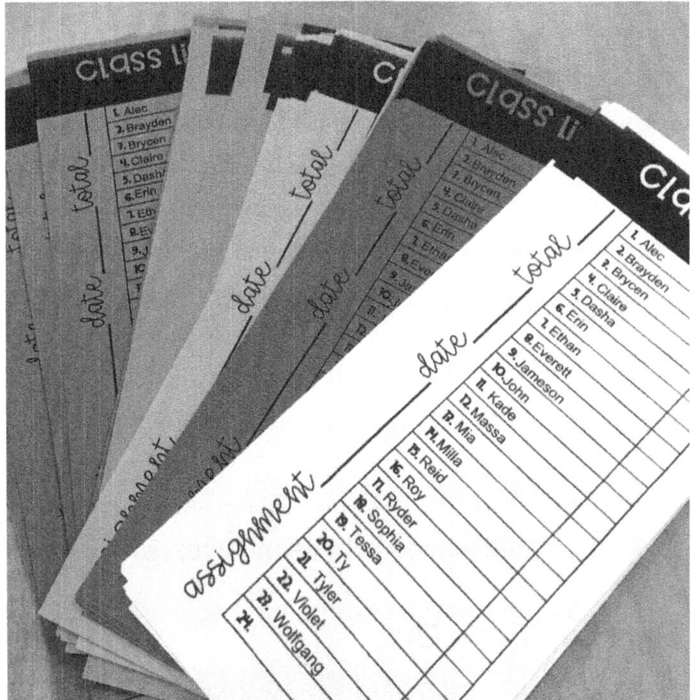

Figure 10.1   Color-coded grading list allows you to return work faster
Courtesy of Easy Teaching Tools, LLC

187

Organization Systems to Save Time Grading

I also used these lists to write notes on them during small groups or as I was grading writing and tucked them away so I could include the note on progress reports, report cards, or emails.

Efficient Grading

This typically ruffles some feathers and that's okay. Believe it or not, you don't have to grade everything because you only have 24 hours in a day. While I understand that some teachers believe *"if it's assigned, it should be graded,"* I want to push back on that. I get where this comes from because it feels like grading everything shows students and parents that you're holding kids accountable and that the work matters. But here's the truth:

> *Grading every single assignment doesn't make you a better teacher, and it doesn't make your students learn more.*

What it does is burn you out, bury you in paper piles, and keep you stuck in an endless cycle of catching up.

Instead of grading everything, shift the belief to this: *"If it's assigned, it has a purpose."* Sometimes that purpose is practice, sometimes it's feedback, and sometimes it's assessment. Not everything needs to go in the gradebook for it to matter. When you stop grading every single thing, you'll find you actually have more time to focus on the assignments that truly reflect student learning and your feedback will be faster and more meaningful.

How does it feel hearing this?

In my classroom, I only graded quizzes, unit tests, writing process pieces, and comprehension assessments. Everything else was spot checked or reviewed together with students. When I stopped grading homework, I saved one hour every single week on this task alone. This system gave me back hours of time and kept the grading piles manageable.

Choose One Part to Focus On

Instead, choose what is most important and let that guide your grading. For example, if you are assessing writing, focus on one part such as introductions or using evidence, not the entire paper. As a teacher, you already know how daunting grading writing can

The Organized Teacher Toolkit

be, so imagine how it feels to receive that back as a six-year-old. When you're looking at math work, grade the problem-solving process instead of every question. Or simply pick three or four problems to correct together as a class, have students write their score at the top of their paper and line up in number order, and as they walk out the door, you record their score on your grading list as they put their work in their cubby. You'll get immediate feedback and see who needs extra support during small groups tomorrow and you just saved at least 30 minutes of grading and filing work! Are you starting to see how powerful this is? The big shift is to focus only on one part instead of everything. This frees you from feeling like you must grade every page that comes across your desk.

Get Students to Help

You do not have to do grading alone. There are simple ways to involve students and lighten your load. Plus, getting students involved allows them to get feedback right away! While I wanted to pull out my hair and began to question all of my life decisions as I taught my kindergarteners how to correct their Word Study or math facts at first with their correcting marker, it paid off in the long run and saved time! It is possible to do it even with the youngest students.

- *Explicitly train your students* with a clear system so they can check their own work during centers or review with partners to hold them accountable.

- *Use answer keys* posted at stations so students can correct as they go. If you're worried about students being dishonest during this process, use this system as a learning opportunity with your students. I always let them know that *they weren't experts yet* and being able to see how they did on an activity let me know what I needed to do as a teacher to support and help them.

- *Technology tools like Seesaw* make it easy for students to submit work that is self-checked or quickly reviewed. I let caregivers know that I was simply "liking" the center work that was turned in and wasn't giving detailed feedback. If there was a glaring issue, I'd leave a comment or respond with audio or video with a reminder and check in with the student later to correct it.

Organization Systems to Save Time Grading

You can even enlist trusted former students or volunteers to help with tasks like sorting papers or stamping simple assignments. When you share responsibility, you save time and help students take ownership of their learning.

Not Everything Needs Lengthy Feedback

One of the biggest grading time savers is realizing that not every assignment requires detailed feedback. Sometimes a check mark, a score, or a happy face with a smelly marker is not only enough, it's more effective. Students benefit most from timely feedback, not lengthy feedback. A stack of essays that takes you three weeks to grade and comment on loses its impact by the time students get it back. On the other hand, a simple score with one targeted comment, returned the next day, helps students connect your feedback directly to what they just learned.

But here's the bigger question: does this assignment actually need feedback at all? Giving feedback takes time and energy, so it's important to think about the ROI (return on investment). In other words, where will your feedback have the most impact on student growth?

I once worked with a teacher who was spending hours giving detailed notes on cursive handwriting assignments. The reality? Students didn't need her personalized feedback on every loop and slant, they just needed consistent practice. Her time would have been better spent giving feedback on comprehension strategies or problem-solving skills that truly mattered for student learning.

A good rule of thumb: focus your feedback where it drives learning, not just compliance.

Here are a few ways to simplify feedback while still keeping it meaningful:

- **Use Symbols or Codes**

    Instead of writing the same notes again and again, create a simple code system: "C" for capitalization, "Sp" for spelling, "E" for evidence. Provide a key so students can self-correct quickly.

The Organized Teacher Toolkit

- **Highlight or Circle Patterns**

  Instead of marking every single mistake, circle one or two examples and have students fix the rest. They'll learn more from correcting their own errors than from seeing every mistake marked.

- **Verbal or Audio Feedback**

  Walk around during centers and give students quick, in-the-moment feedback. Or use tools like Mote, which is a free Chrome extension, to record 20-second audio comments. Students love hearing your voice, and you save time writing.

- **Quick Exit Tickets**

  Instead of grading every practice page, give a one-question exit ticket. Sort them into "Got It" and "Needs Review." This gives both you and your students immediate feedback without a huge stack of grading.

High Return on Investment = Give Feedback

- *Writing pieces tied to standards*

  Imagine how overwhelmed students must feel receiving writing back when everything is graded, especially for emerging writers. Focus on just one or two standards so that students develop a deeper understanding rather than trying to cover everything at once.

- *Assessments that show mastery of key concepts*

  These are quick checks, quizzes, and assessments that help you see whether students truly grasp the essential skills you've taught. They give you concrete data so you can adjust instruction, reteach as needed, or confidently move forward.

- *Projects or performance tasks that reflect deeper understanding*

  These larger tasks allow students to apply what they've learned in meaningful ways, showing not just what they know but how they think. They also give you a clearer picture of students' reasoning, creativity, and ability to connect concepts to real-world situations.

Organization Systems to Save Time Grading

Low ROI = Keep It Minimal

- *Daily practice worksheets and center work*

  A quick check is good enough to check for quick understanding or completion.

- *Repetitive drills like handwriting or fact practice*

  These tasks build fluency through repetition, so they don't need detailed comments. Your students just need consistent practice. A quick check for completion is usually enough, freeing up your time for more meaningful feedback elsewhere.

- *Warm-ups or exit tickets (use for quick data, not long comments)*

  These are designed to give you a fast snapshot of where students are, not to become mini essays you grade in depth. Skim them for patterns, adjust your instruction if needed, and move on—no lengthy notes required.

Tip: Before you pick up your grading pen, ask yourself: *Will this feedback move student learning forward?* If the answer is no, keep it quick and move on. Oftentimes, a stamp or smiley face with a smelly marker does the job!

When you put your energy into the assignments that truly matter, your feedback is more meaningful, students grow faster, and you save hours every week.

Once you've shifted your mindset about what really needs feedback, the next step is finding tools and strategies that make the feedback you *do* give faster and easier. The good news is there are countless ways to cut down your grading time without sacrificing quality. From rubrics to tech tools to peer support, these additional strategies will help you work smarter, not harder, when it comes to grading.

Additional Time-Saving Grading Strategies and Tools

1. Rubrics and Single-Point Rubrics

- Instead of writing lengthy comments on every paper, use a simple rubric. A traditional rubric is great when you need consistency across your grade level

The Organized Teacher Toolkit

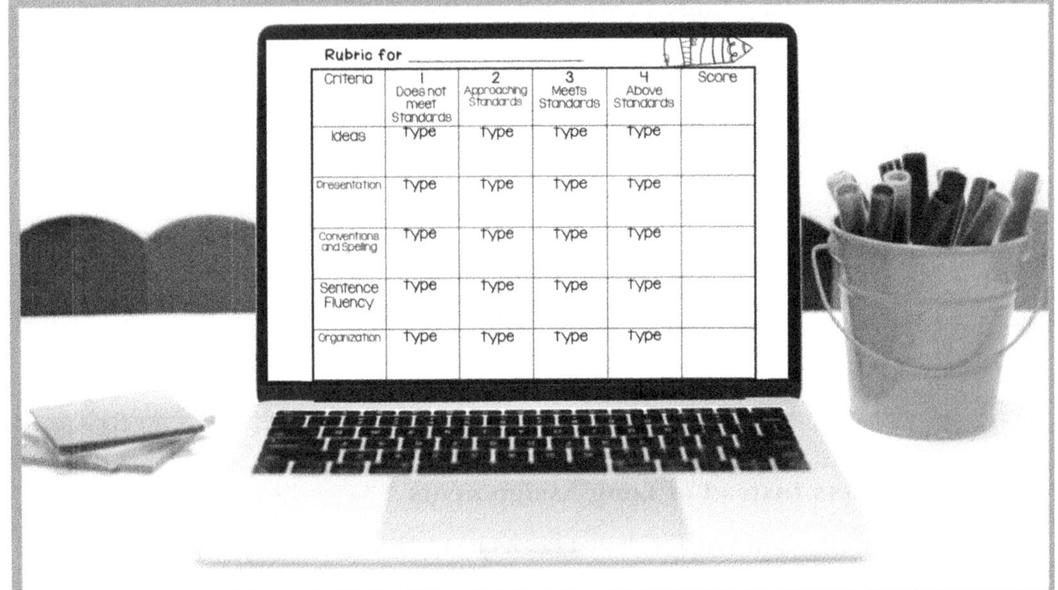

Figure 10.2 Editable rubric

Scan to get this download

to keep everyone aligned, which reduces interpretation and bias. It also has clearly defined performance levels and gives feedback without having to write a lot. Download the editable rubric shown in Figure 10.2 to use with your grade level and students.

- **A single-point rubric** (listing just the target expectation with space for notes) saves time and focuses feedback on growth. Instead of evaluating multiple standards, you're looking at just one, which is also less overwhelming for your students.

2. **Digital Grading Tools**

- **Google Classroom** or **Microsoft Teams** let you create rubrics and reuse comments with a click.

- **Autograde quizzes** using Google Forms or platforms like Quizizz, Edpuzzle, or Socrative. They grade automatically and give instant feedback to students. Inside The Organized Teacher Club, teachers have access to Google Form templates to quickly use and assign to their own students.

Organization Systems to Save Time Grading

3. Comment Banks / Copy-Paste Comments

- Create a "comment bank" of your most common feedback phrases.

- Store them in Google Docs, Google Classroom, or grading apps so you can paste instead of rewriting.

4. Exit Tickets Instead of Long Assignments

- Use short exit tickets for daily checks instead of grading every practice page. Collect a snapshot of understanding without adding to your pile. You can easily record the grade and jot any notes on your grading list.

5. Peer Review and Self-Assessment

- Students can swap papers for peer feedback (with clear checklists), based on your district's grading policy, and give feedback on writing.

- Self-assessment checklists encourage reflection and reduce the need for you to grade every step.

6. Color-Coding and Quick Checks

- Use highlighters or stamps to mark key strengths/areas for improvement instead of lengthy notes. A quick "traffic light system" (green = good, yellow = needs a little work, pink = revisit) can replace detailed comments.

7. Tech Tools for Feedback

- **Mote** (free voice comments in Google Classroom/Docs).

- **Kaizena** (free audio and text feedback for Google Docs).

- **Seesaw** (students upload work, you can respond with quick audio/video feedback).

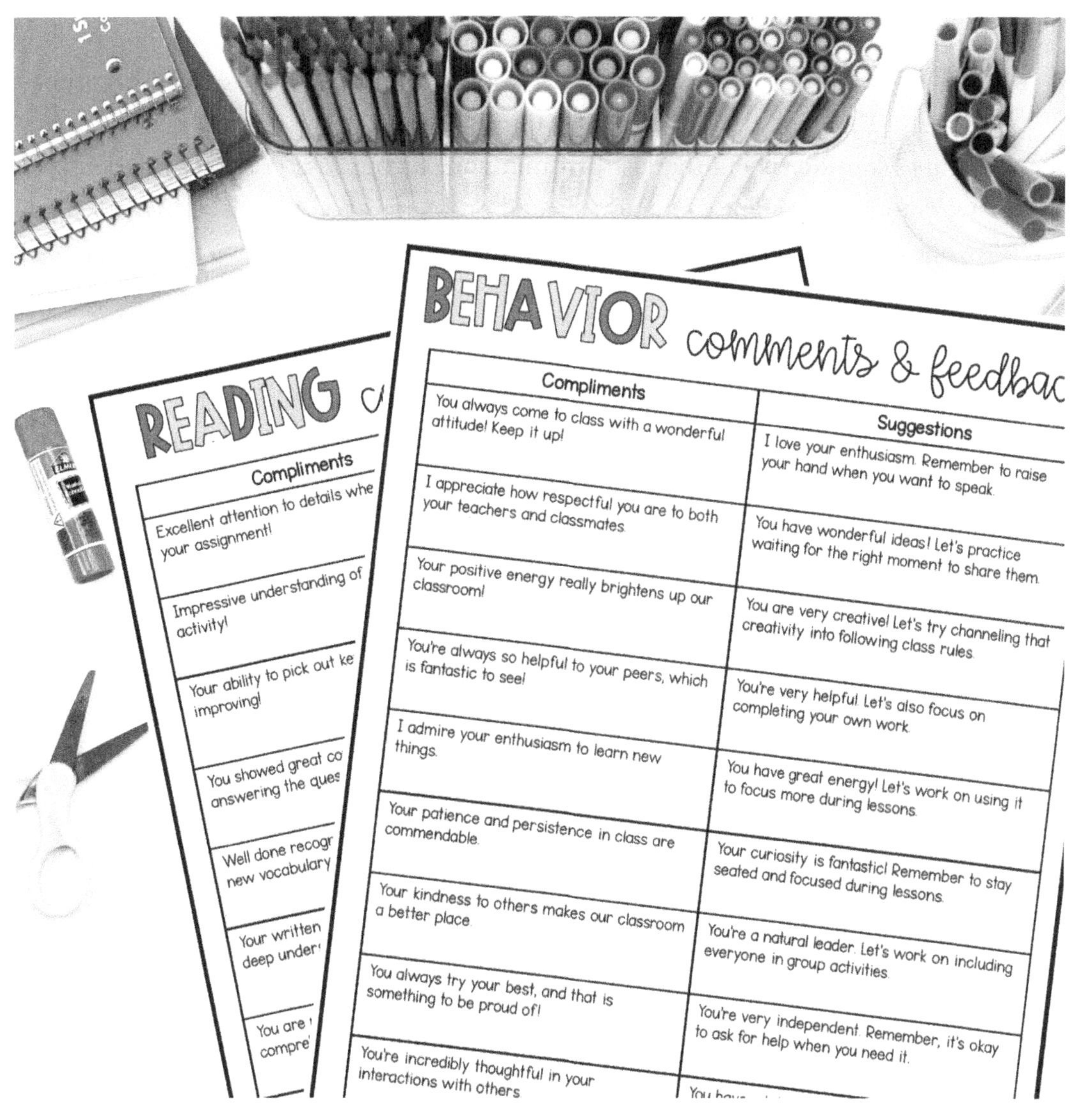

Figure 10.3 Comment bank to save teachers time with feedback and report cards

Organization Systems to Save Time Grading

8. Grade with Students in Real Time

Review work during small groups or conferences so feedback happens immediately. This cuts down your take-home load and gives instant clarity to students. Consider using the last five minutes of your lesson after students have worked independently to grade several problems as a class under the doc cam while students use a correcting marker to follow along. They can line up and hold their paper up to their chest with their score circled while you quickly record their score on your grading list.

9. Weighted Grading

Give more weight to assessments and projects, less to daily practice. This way, you don't feel pressured to grade every worksheet but still capture progress in the gradebook.

10. Use Volunteers or Former Students

Train classroom aides, parent volunteers, or even former students to help with simple grading tasks like checking multiple-choice answers, depending on your school's grading policy.

Grading will always be part of teaching, but it doesn't have to take over your evenings, weekends, and peace of mind. The key is shifting your mindset: not every assignment needs detailed feedback, and not everything even needs to be graded. When you focus on what truly matters, use efficient systems, and lean on tools and strategies that save time, you give yourself the freedom to stay caught up without carrying stacks of papers home.

The best part? When you stop drowning in grading, you're able to return work faster, give feedback that actually helps students grow, and reclaim the energy you need for teaching and for life outside of school.

Task: Which grading time saver will you try first this week to take back your time and make feedback more meaningful for your students?

exxxistence/
Adobe Stock Photo

Chapter 11

Classroom Organization Systems

You've learned how to set boundaries, manage your time, clear the clutter, and create a functional space that's backed by research. You've streamlined lesson planning, discovered grading time savers, and built habits that protect your evenings and weekends. Now it's time for the final piece, the classroom organization systems that pull it all together and keep your classroom running smoothly day after day.

This chapter is the most exciting because these are the systems that make organization sustainable, not just a one-time fix. With the right routines in place, every paper, every supply, and every task has a home. Things flow more easily, your classroom feels calmer, and you finally have the freedom to focus on what matters most: teaching your students.

And here's the best part, you don't have to wait until next school year to feel the difference. You can start building these systems right now. With a little consistency, you'll walk out of your classroom each day knowing you did your very best, confident that everything has its place, and free to actually enjoy your life outside of school.

This is where the overwhelm ends and the flow begins so your class can run like a well-oiled machine. I did all the trial-and-error for you to save you some time so let's dive in.

Teaching and Learning Systems

At the heart of every classroom is teaching and learning. But planning, collecting, and tracking student work can quickly snowball if you don't have a clear system. These tools help you stay on top of lessons and student progress without burning out.

Daily Lessons

One of the biggest game changers in my own classroom was ditching the traditional teacher desk and creating intentional spaces for the things I used every single day. Instead of letting a desk turn into a catch-all for piles of "stuff," I relied on three main areas, my planning corner, my main teaching table, and my guided reading table. Each spot had a clear purpose, which meant I always knew where to go when I needed something, and my classroom stayed so much calmer.

The centerpiece of this system was my three-tiered tray at my main teaching table. This tray became my command center. On the top tier went my lesson plans and any materials I needed for the day. The middle tier was my "not yet" space—items I didn't get to that day but wanted close at hand. At the end of the day, I'd take those materials from the middle tray and decide where they belonged, often filing them into my weekly paper sorter to use later in the week. The bottom tier held the daily things I used all year to model under the doc cam like my Word Study and interactive math note book, dictionary, and more. Because everything had a designated home within the tray, I wasn't scrambling mid-lesson or wasting energy hunting things down.

This system also gave me a built-in prep routine. Before I left for the day, I'd pull the activities from my paper sorter from Chapter 9 for the next day and place them on the top tier of the tray. That way, when I walked into the classroom the following morning, I was instantly ready to teach without the stress of gathering materials on the fly. Over time, this routine saved me countless minutes each day and modeled organization for my students. They saw me use the trays consistently and began to understand that staying organized isn't about perfection, it's about having reliable routines that keep learning flowing smoothly (see Figure 11.1).

Passing Out and Collecting Student Work

One of the most overwhelming parts of teaching is managing the sheer volume of student work. With 25 students and multiple assignments a day, it can feel like you're drowning in papers. That's why I teach a system I learned from Rick Morris that simplifies both passing out and collecting work. It starts with one simple tool: a bell (see Figure 11.2). Instead of me handing out every worksheet or constantly repeating directions, the bell became our paper signal. I'd ring it once, and the

The Organized Teacher Toolkit

Figure 11.1　Three-tiered tray for daily copies

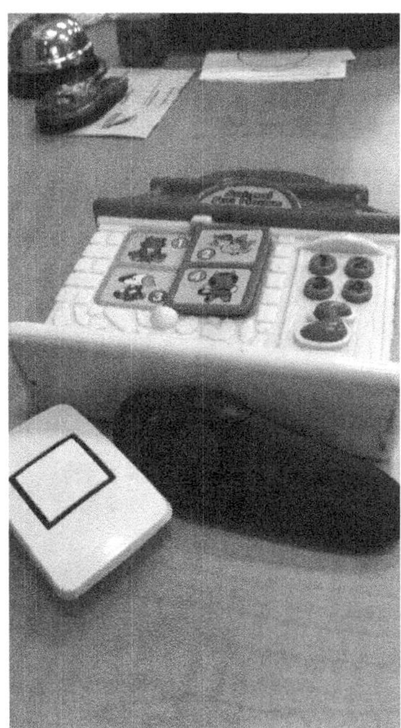

Figure 11.2　Bell system to easily pass out papers

Classroom Organization Systems

designated student from each group would come up, hold up the number of fingers for how many copies their group needed, and return to pass them out. Not only did this save me from wasting my voice, it also gave students ownership and cut down on transition time.

For collecting work, I relied on two baskets: one large flat basket labeled "Important Stuff" and one plastic, stand-up magazine holder with numbered file folders. The numbered basket was our "Turn-In" basket, used specifically for center work. Each student had a number, and when they finished an activity, they slipped their paper into their numbered folder. This eliminated the no-name problem (if it's in folder #12, I know it belongs to student #12), and it also gave me a quick way to scan at the end of the day to see who had turned in work and who still had gaps. The "Important Stuff" basket was for items that required my immediate attention: assessments, quizzes, permission slips, or parent notes from home. Students knew that if something really mattered, it went straight there (see Figures 11.3 and 11.4).

Figure 11.3 "Important stuff" basket for assessments and notes from home

The Organized Teacher Toolkit

Figure 11.4   Numbered "turn-in" basket for center work

Scan to get this download

This two-basket system streamlined everything. No more piles of papers handed to me while I was teaching, no more digging through random stacks on my desk, and no more "I swear I turned it in!" conversations. To reinforce the habit, I even attached a highlighter to the Turn-In basket, so students got in the routine of highlighting their name before dropping their work inside. Over time, this system became second nature. Students knew where everything belonged, I saved time (and sanity) during transitions, and I could easily keep on top of who was turning things in and who wasn't without ever raising my voice or chasing down stray papers. Plus, I was no longer drowning in all of the paperwork because center work was no longer mixed in with assessments and notes from home.

Sending Work Home

Once you've passed out, collected, and graded student work, the next challenge is getting it home in an organized way. Without a system, papers end up crumpled in backpacks, lost in desks, or forgotten entirely. That's why I rely on two tools that make this process smooth and predictable: student cubbies and the Return to School folder. Together, these create a routine that students, families, and I can count on every single week.

In my classroom, I designated one day, which was Friday, as "take home day." That's when all graded work, assessments, and notes from the office went home at once. Each student had a cubby (for several years I used a fancy cubby-set that was gifted to me and then moved to a simple shoe organizer from the hardware store). Throughout the week, papers got tucked inside their cubbies (see Figure 11.5). On Friday afternoons, students gathered their stack and transferred it into their Return to

Figure 11.5 Student cubbies to take work and paper home

School folder. At first, I gave us a solid 20 minutes for this routine, since it takes practice to teach students how to collect papers carefully and not drop them along the way. Over time, it became automatic, and I could shorten the process, but in the beginning, that extra time saved both me and my students a lot of frustration.

The true hero of this system is the Return to School folder, or what my students affectionately called their "black folder." This durable, two-pocket folder is labeled "Return to School" on one side and "Keep at Home" on the other. Each morning, students placed it on their desks, and if they had permission slips, signed forms, or notes from home, those went in the Return to School pocket and got placed into the "Important Stuff" bin. At the end of the day, anything finished that needed to go home went in the Keep at Home side. If something was unfinished or required a parent signature, it went into the Return to School side and came back the next day. This one tool eliminated confusion, cut down on wasted transition time, and gave parents and caregivers a clear, reliable system for checking their child's work (see Figure 11.6).

Figure 11.6   A student folder to send work home

Over the years, I've tried other methods such as laminated folders, large plastic envelopes, even sending papers loose in backpacks, but nothing comes close to the Return to School folder. It's durable, simple, and worth every penny (around $3 each, or cheaper if ordered in bulk). Families love it because they know exactly where to look for important items, and I love it because I'm no longer scrambling to figure out if something made it home. With cubbies feeding into the folder and one consistent day for take-home work, this system turns a chaotic paper shuffle into an organized, dependable routine.

Student Assessments and Grading

Now that you've established a system for sending student work home consistently, the next question becomes: *what about assessments?* Graded tests and quizzes often feel like their own category because they're high-stakes, parents want to see them, and you need to keep records for grading. Without a plan, these papers can become another overwhelming pile. Here's the system that has kept teachers inside The Organized Teacher Club on top of assessments year after year.

Assessments and Grading (From Basket to Cubbies)

In my classroom, all assessments went straight into the Important Stuff basket as soon as students turned them in. From there, I'd clip the assessments together with a grading sheet and move them into my designated Grading drawer from the three-drawer system. Sometimes I graded them myself; other times, if it was an assignment that could be checked by a parent volunteer, I'd place it in the "Parent" file at the back table. Having a consistent landing spot meant I never had to wonder where those important papers were.

Once assessments were graded, I didn't immediately rush to input every score. Instead, I batched the process. I kept my grading lists paper clipped to the assessments and stored in my grading drawer until I had time to sit down and enter multiple scores at once in our online gradebook. To make this easier, I color-coded grading sheets so that when it came time to input grades, I could find exactly what I needed quickly. This batching method saved me from the constant disruption of entering grades piecemeal throughout the week.

The Organized Teacher Toolkit

After grades were recorded, I placed the stack of graded assessments in the back of our Turn-In basket by the cubbies. The papers stuck up slightly as a visual reminder to the student helpers who were in charge of filing that they were ready to be put away. During our daily classroom jobs, two students were responsible for filing assessments and work into the cubbies. By Friday, all assessments were waiting in the right cubbies, ready to head home with the rest of the weekly work.

Of course, there were exceptions. If we graded something together in class like a phonics quiz or comprehension check, sometimes I let students place it directly in their Return to School folders and take it home that day. Other times, I'd have them resubmit it into the Important Stuff basket so I could quickly double-check their accuracy and note who needed extra support. And other times, they would put it in their cubby. Flexibility is key here. The system gave me structure but also allowed me to adapt depending on the class or the type of assessment. What mattered most was that assessments never turned into a mystery pile on my desk; they always had a next step.

If you need to hang onto assessments or important work, you most likely have a filing system already. If you don't, consider using a milk crate and hanging file folders. To save time, use number order so you can use them over and over. You can easily file (or enlist help) student assessments quickly to refer back to later during conferences, Student Study Teams (SSTs), or other important meetings.

Absent and Unfinished Work

After assessments, another big question teachers ask is: *What do I do with absent and unfinished work?* Without a system, both can quickly pile up and create stress for you and your students. That's why I teach two simple routines: one for absent students and one for unfinished work that saves time, keeps parents and caregivers in the loop, and puts responsibility back on students.

When it comes to absent students, I believe in assigning the missed work. My mindset is simple: if families choose to take vacations during the school year, I still want them to see the amount of learning we do each day. To keep it manageable, I created a system using a bright-colored Absent Work Note (ours were always orange or hot pink so they stood out). Whenever a student missed a day, I listed the assignments, the date, and when the work was due (see Figure 11.7). I clipped the note to their stack of assignments using a binder clip and placed it in their Return to School folder. Caregivers knew exactly what

Classroom Organization Systems

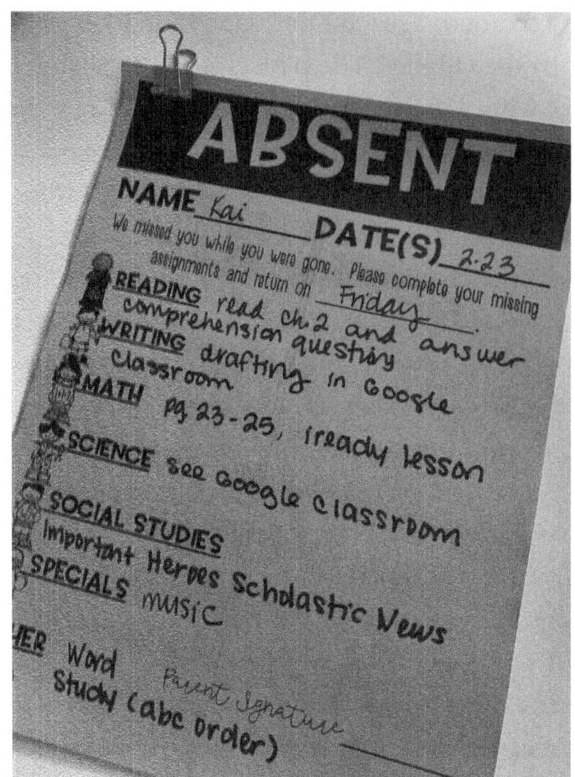

Figure 11.7 An absent work note to keep track of work

to expect because I explained the process at Back to School Night, and the bright color made it easy for them to notice right away. Once completed, the student simply returned the packet to the Important Stuff basket, which kept everything streamlined.

Unfinished work is another beast that can easily eat up your time if you don't have a clear plan. I tried various systems, ketchup folders in desks and unfinished bins but they created more work for me because I had to micromanage it. What finally worked was the clipboard system. Every student had a clipboard that stayed on their desk all year long (see Figure 11.8). Whenever an assignment wasn't finished, it went straight onto their clipboard. That way, I could glance around the room and instantly see who had work piling up. This visibility gave me insight into why it wasn't being finished—was it too hard, was the student distracted, or were they just being perfectionists? Having the clipboard in plain sight made it easier to identify patterns and support students.

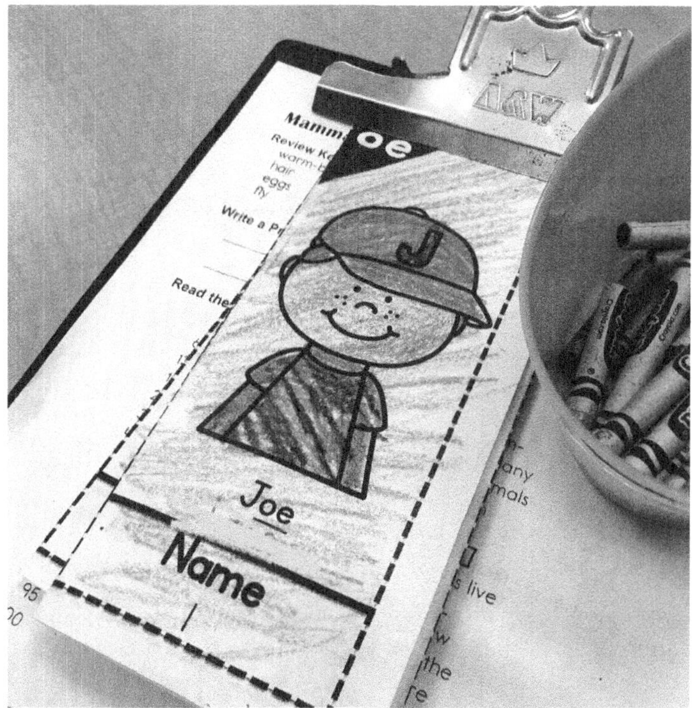

Figure 11.8 How to use a clipboard for unfinished work
Courtesy of Easy Teaching Tools, LLC

To build accountability, I created a routine around making up unfinished work. During our daily read-aloud after recess, students with unfinished assignments knew to quietly work at their desk while still listening to the story. If they still hadn't completed the work by the end of the week, they had to use Fun Friday time to catch up. Nobody wants to miss Fun Friday, so this motivated most students to stay on top of things. For chronic unfinished work, I used a bright pink "Oops Note" that went home stapled to the incomplete assignments (see Figure 11.9). The note listed reasons like "I was talking," "I didn't use my time wisely," or "I didn't understand." Parents signed it over the weekend, and everything came back Monday in the Return to School folder. This system not only kept students accountable but also created a paper trail I could use if I needed to meet with families or hold a conference. Over time, unfinished work became the exception instead of the rule, all because of one simple clipboard and a brightly colored note.

Scan to get this download

Figure 11.9   Oops note for unfinished work

Classroom Environment and Supplies

Your space sets the tone for learning. Systems for supplies and technology help you avoid daily chaos and give students ownership.

Running Out of Supplies

If you've ever been in the middle of a great lesson, only to be interrupted by a student whose glue stick just died or whose scissors broke, you know how quickly lost supplies can derail learning. After a few too many interruptions like that, I knew I needed a better way. I needed one that built student independence while protecting my teaching time. That's when I created our student-managed supply area. Instead of 24 kids coming to me for replacements, they became problem-solvers who knew exactly where to go when something ran out.

The supply area is simple: it's one designated space in the classroom stocked with the essentials my students use regularly. Over the years, mine has included staplers, tape, publishing pencils, revising and editing markers, Expo markers and erasers, Sharpies for art projects, glue sticks (always a hot commodity), scissors, and highlighters. I organized

everything in a basket with smaller containers from the Target Dollar Spot or Dollar Tree to keep it tidy. The key is stocking only the supplies students will actually run out of throughout the year. If it's something you use only a handful of times, it doesn't need to live in the supply station (see Figure 11.10).

Of course, even a well-stocked supply area will eventually run out so I built a system for that too. Students are taught from day one that if they take the last item (say, the last glue stick), it's their responsibility to let me know. Sometimes I'd restock it

Figure 11.10   Student supply area for when they run out of common supplies

Classroom Organization Systems

myself, but often I'd have that student grab a handful of replacements from our Sterilite supply bins—the ones where I stored all the extras families brought in at the start of the year—and replenish the supply area. That way, only one student was involved in restocking, not the entire class stopping instruction. This system not only preserved my teaching time, but it also gave students a sense of ownership and responsibility. They loved that they could solve their own supply problems without waiting on me, and I loved that I could keep teaching without constant interruptions. Over time, it became one of the most seamless, sanity-saving routines in our classroom.

Once your running out of supplies system is in place, the next area that needs equal attention is math. Between manipulatives, dice, flashcards, and games, the materials can multiply fast. Without a clear organization system, you'll find yourself wasting time hunting down supplies or dealing with noisy distractions. Setting up a streamlined math area not only saves your sanity, but also gives students independence during centers and rotations.

Math Manipulatives and Dice (Simple Storage + Noise-Free Rolling)

For manipulatives, I relied on a hanging shoe organizer nailed to the wall. Each pocket held a different tool my students needed regularly: dice, rubber bands for games, paper clips for spinners, flashcards, game pieces, Unifix cubes, or 3D shapes (see Figure 11.11). Because everything was clearly visible and within reach, students didn't need to interrupt me at the guided math table to ask where supplies were. Consider even adding paperclips to one of the pockets for students to grab when playing a spinner game. It will save you so much time since you won't have to pass out and collect them. They knew exactly where to go, and just as importantly, exactly where to return items when they were done. Over the years, this system kept our math area clutter-free and made rotations run smoothly.

One of my favorite hacks for math centers was using magnetic spice containers for foam dice (see Figure 11.12). If you've ever had 25 kids rolling plastic dice on desks at once, you know the noise is enough to give you a headache. Instead of having students toss dice across the table, I placed a single die inside each spice container. The clear lid let students see the number after they shook it, but the die never left the container. No more dice flying across the room, no more loud clattering on desks, and no wasted time crawling under tables to retrieve runaway dice. My students loved the novelty of it, and I loved the peace and order it brought to our centers.

Figure 11.11 Math manipulatives storage students can access

Figure 11.12 Easy dice storage in magnetic containers

With manipulatives organized and dice contained, math rotations became more about the learning and less about the logistics. Students had the tools they needed right at their fingertips, and I could focus on teaching instead of managing supplies. Little systems like these may seem small, but they add up to a huge difference in classroom flow and student independence.

Technology

After establishing systems for supplies, the next piece of classroom organization to consider is technology. Devices are amazing tools for learning, but without clear routines, they can turn into one more source of chaos. From headphones to Chromebooks to classroom computers, the right systems keep everything working smoothly and save you from constant interruptions.

The first step in organizing technology is to decide how you want devices stored and managed. In my classroom, I used different setups depending on what we had—letter trays with a power strip for charging, labeled baskets with dividers, and even a Chromebook cart. The key was always consistency: every device had a number, and students were trained to put it back in the right spot. To make this even clearer, I used washi tape to color-code devices and their storage slots. If Chromebook #7 had navy tape, it matched the navy-labeled slot in the cart. Students knew immediately where things belonged, and I didn't waste energy playing detective with missing devices.

Headphones were another challenge. After dealing with lice outbreaks one year, I moved away from shared headphones and had each student bring in their own. For families who couldn't, I provided $1 earbuds from Dollar Tree because they were inexpensive, compact, and easy to store. Students wrote their names and numbers on the cases, which kept things organized and prevented mix-ups. For bulkier headphones, a hanging shoe organizer worked perfectly as individual storage pockets. Whether earbuds or over-ear sets, every pair had a home, which cut down on clutter and eliminated wasted time searching.

Finally, I created student ownership through tech helper jobs. Each day, two students were assigned to oversee technology use and organization. They made sure Chromebooks were plugged in, devices were returned to the right spots, and classmates

The Organized Teacher Toolkit

were treating equipment respectfully. If issues arose, they took the lead, sometimes even "shutting down" tech use until peers showed responsibility again. This not only protected our devices but also gave students a sense of pride and accountability. By combining clear storage systems, individual responsibility for headphones, and tech helper roles, technology became a smooth, well-managed part of our daily routine instead of a constant disruption.

Communication and Collaboration

Clear communication reduces stress for both you and your classroom community.

Caregiver Communication

Pick one consistent method (weekly email, app, or newsletter). Stick to the same day each week so families know when to expect updates. This builds trust and prevents scattered "Did you tell us?" questions.

Sub Plans

Emergencies happen, and the last thing you want is to scramble. Keep a "Sub Binder" ready at all times with your seating chart, routines, emergency procedures, and simple lesson templates (see Figure 11.13). Add a quick "Day at a Glance" page so a sub can smoothly step into your shoes.

Daily Transitions and Routines

The little in-between moments can make or break your day. When transitions are predictable, students feel secure and you stay calm.

Dismissal Routine with Music

Choose one song that signals the start of dismissal. Students know it's time to pack up, clean up, and line up. This consistent cue turns a potentially chaotic part of the day into an orderly routine.

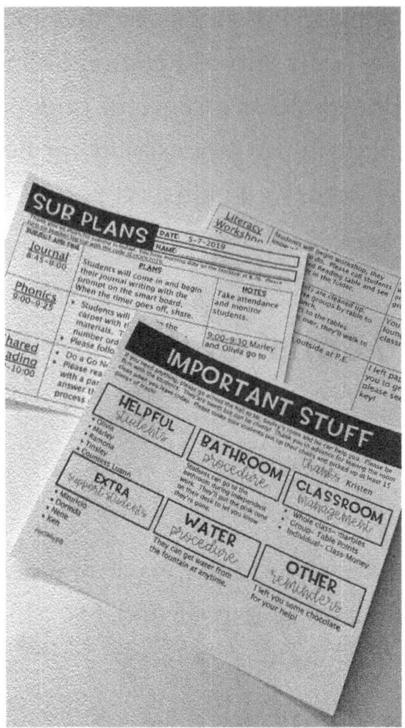

Figure 11.13   The best sub plans to save you time and ensure your plans are followed

Other Transitions

Use quick cues like a chime, call-and-response, or countdown to signal movement between activities. Consistency is key; students shouldn't wonder what comes next.

Catch-All Systems That Save Your Sanity

Some systems don't fit neatly into a category but will save you time and headaches.

Volunteers and Visitors

The most important thing to remember is that volunteers should support what's *already* happening in your classroom, not create busy work. Early in my career, I used to scramble to come up with random tasks when a parent showed up. Now, I make a clear list of where I truly need help, things like fluency practice, leading a small reading group, word study, or comprehension activities. One of my favorite roles is the "copy parent" who takes care of making copies and prepping materials. Once I identified these meaningful jobs, I invited parents to sign up through a Google Form, a Signup Genius, or even a simple note home. From there, I created a weekly schedule so I always knew who was coming in and when.

Once volunteers were scheduled, I set up a filing shelf system with labeled slots for each day of the week. Before the week began, I prepped materials and instructions for the parents in those slots. This way, when Tuesday's volunteer walked in, they could grab the Tuesday folder and know exactly what to do. Each folder included a simple instruction sheet reminding them of confidentiality, expectations for student behavior, incentives to hand out, and a reminder to transition students back quietly. If they were leading groups, the sheet also listed how long each group should run and what activity to do. By being explicit upfront, I eliminated the need for constant interruptions while I was teaching.

To make transitions smoother, I trained parents to call groups by table (for example, "I need Table A") instead of reading off individual names. This kept things calm and efficient. I also provided them with a mini Time Timer so parents could manage the 13-minute group rotations themselves without me stopping my reading group. Parents loved the independence, and students respected that their learning time with volunteers was structured and purposeful. At the end of each session, the entire class would thank the volunteer before they left. That simple act of appreciation not only built a positive classroom culture but also ensured parents felt valued and eager to return.

With this system, parent volunteers became an extension of my classroom routines instead of a distraction. They knew their role, had the materials they needed, and felt supported. I could continue focusing on instruction, and my students benefited from the extra help. The best part? Once the system was in place, it ran itself year after year with very little extra effort from me.

After establishing strong systems for parent volunteers, the next step is empowering the people who are in your classroom every single day—your students. Giving them meaningful jobs not only lightens your workload but also builds responsibility, ownership, and pride in the classroom.

Student Jobs (Ownership + Responsibility)

I can't emphasize this enough: you do not need to do everything for your students. You are not their mom, dad, or grandparent and they are more than capable of helping. In fact, most kids *love* the chance to pitch in and take on responsibilities that keep the classroom running smoothly. Assigning jobs gives them ownership, teaches them accountability, and helps them feel like valued members of your classroom community.

Over the years, I've used a wide range of jobs, from the practical to the fun. Some favorites include: the Light Helper who turns lights on and off during brain breaks or projector use; the Pencil Sharpeners who handle all dull pencils at the end of the day (no more constant interruptions mid-lesson); and the Tech Helpers who support classmates with logging in or solving small Chromebook issues. I've also had students in charge of Cubbies (filing papers, checking for no-name assignments, stamping work), the Library (keeping books organized and neat), and our Centers (making sure all materials and manipulatives are put back in the right place). Even simple jobs like Trash Helper, Lunch Monitor, and Board Eraser gave students pride and took small but important tasks off my plate.

To implement this system, I spent the first week of school introducing jobs two at a time and modeling expectations. On Friday, students selected their job choices (with the understanding that not everyone would get their first pick). I used Popsicle sticks or a job chart to assign roles, and jobs rotated about every two months which was long enough for students to really learn and take pride in the role, but not so long that it became stale. To signal job time each day, I set a three- to four-minute song as our cue. Students knew that when the song came on, it was time to complete their responsibilities before dismissal. If they finished their job before the song was over, they knew to pick up any trash on the ground. This was the same for everyone so it kept students on task without asking me what to do next! To ensure this happens even when you have a sub, see if you have an old iPhone around and leave that in your classroom. It doesn't need data or to even be used except for setting the alarm to go off at the end of the day to signal the start of jobs. I learned this the hard way

What jobs would help your classroom run better?

once when I was at the district office for a training and my job alarm for my students went off because it was programmed on my own phone which did my students no good.

The key is to be clear and consistent. Jobs should never feel like busywork, they should directly support the flow of your classroom. With modeling, accountability, and a little structure, students not only rise to the occasion but often exceed your expectations. I've found that my students loved their jobs so much that they held each other accountable for doing them well. When kids feel ownership over the classroom environment, it transforms the space into a community and it frees you up to focus on what matters most: teaching.

> **Tip:** To cut down on transitions and another thing you have to do, consider rotating jobs once a month or once every other month to save your sanity, trust me!

> ### Real Teacher Talk
>
> When it comes to things like how I do sub plans or organize students and their jobs, I oftentimes get comments from other teachers on liking the way that I do things. —Melissa W.

Emergency and Seasonal Prep

Create a "just in case" folder with emergency sub work, indoor recess ideas, and seasonal supplies (like tissues and sanitizer). You'll thank yourself later when the cold season hits.

Number Order

Placing students in number order will save you hours of time during the school year! You can do this by alphabetical order by first name. Remember, this will be flexible the first week or two of school in case students leave or join your class. When a new

Classroom Organization Systems

student joins your class later in the year, simply add them to the last number. Students can line up in number order, which means lining up is faster and easier for emergency drills, walking to lunch, sitting on the carpet, and more! Plus, to save time, your bulletin boards with student work will also be numbered, which makes putting up work easier.

Tip: This tip I learned from Rick Morris of New Management, one of the best PD presenters before he retired. He suggested to put your students in number order by first name because it's a lot easier to remember first names alphabetically than it is last names. Your online gradebook should also let you sort your class list by first name as well so it makes it easy to input grades from your grading list.

By now, you have seen how a handful of simple, consistent systems can transform the way your classroom runs. From daily lessons and student work to supplies, technology, math manipulatives, volunteers, and jobs, each of these routines gives you back precious time and mental energy. Just as importantly, they give your students ownership, independence, and a sense of calm predictability.

The goal is not to adopt every system at once or to copy mine exactly. The goal is to choose the ones that fit you, your teaching style, and your students. Start with the area that feels the most overwhelming right now. Maybe it is piles of student work, or maybe it is running out of glue sticks in the middle of a lesson. Put just one system in place. Once it becomes part of your daily flow, add another. Step by step, you will create a classroom that feels organized, efficient, and joyful instead of cluttered and stressful.

These systems do more than make your day easier. They also ripple outward. Students learn responsibility, parents feel included and informed, and substitutes walk into a space that already has structure. Everyone knows their role and is able to help. When that happens, you get to spend more time on what matters most: connecting with kids and teaching in ways that bring you joy.

So as you close this chapter, take a deep breath and remember that you do not need to do it all and you do not need to do it alone. With clear, purposeful systems in place, you will not only protect yourself from burnout but also create the kind of classroom where both you and your students can thrive.

exxxistence/
Adobe Stock Photo

Task:

- Which system from this chapter feels the most urgent for you to put into place?

- What small step can you take this week to begin setting it up?

- How will this system save you time, energy, or stress once it is up and running?

Take a few minutes to jot down your answers. When you return to your classroom tomorrow, commit to starting with just one system. Small, consistent changes add up to big results.

Classroom Organization Systems

Conclusion: This Is Your Moment

If there is one thing I want you to take from this book, it is this: you are doing a better job than you think. If you've made it to the end of this book, pause for a second and let that sink in. You carved out time between lesson planning, parent emails, data meetings, snack duty, and the thousand unseen tasks that keep your classroom running. You showed up for yourself, page after page. And that alone tells me something important: you are ready for change.

Not the kind of change that requires burning everything down and starting from scratch. Not the Pinterest-perfect version of teaching that people outside our field seem to imagine. I mean real change—sustainable, practical, soul-protecting change. The kind that allows you to breathe again. The kind that lets you walk out of school while it's still light out. The kind that gives you back your evenings, your weekends, your joy.

You didn't read this book by accident. Something in you is craving a different way of teaching and a different way of living. And I want you to hear this clearly: You are capable of creating it.

One of the biggest shifts teachers tell me they make after working with the Organized Teacher System is realizing they were never the problem. The system—both the literal school system and the invisible rules you've absorbed over time trains teachers to accept overload as normal. It conditions you to believe exhaustion is part of the job description, boundaries are optional, and your worth is measured by how much you sacrifice. But throughout this book, you've seen the truth: teaching becomes sustainable when you stop trying to do everything and start doing the right things.

You've learned how to name your core values so you can prioritize what matters. You've learned how to set boundaries that protect your time, energy, and emotional space. You've learned how to build simple systems that make the day flow instead of fracturing it, how to manage your workload with intention instead of urgency, and how to reduce the mental clutter so there's space for creativity again. You've learned how to leave school at school, not because you're lazy or uncaring, but because you deserve a full life outside your classroom. This work isn't about perfection. It's about permission—the permission to choose differently.

At the heart of everything you've read is The Organized Teacher System, built on four essential pillars that work together to make this kind of teaching possible: time management and boundaries, a clutter-free space, and simple organization systems. These pillars aren't meant to be tackled all at once or mastered overnight. They're designed to support each other, which means when one pillar strengthens, the others become easier. Clear boundaries protect your time so your systems actually get used. A clutter-free space reduces mental overload so planning feels manageable. Strong routines reduce decision fatigue so your days run more smoothly. When these four pillars are in place, even imperfectly, teaching stops feeling like constant triage and starts feeling intentional again.

Every teacher I've coached has had a moment—sometimes small, sometimes seismic—where they finally see the possibility of a different future. For some, it's the first time they leave school by 4 p.m. and realize nothing fell apart. For others, it's saying no without explaining or apologizing. Sometimes it's organizing one tiny area of the classroom and feeling something unlock inside. Maybe you've felt your own version of that as you read these pages. That spark? That shift? That quiet voice saying, *I think I can actually do this. . .*—that's your aha moment. That's the beginning. And beginnings matter more than anything else.

This work doesn't require you to have everything figured out. You don't need a color-coded calendar for every hour of the week or a classroom that looks like a catalog. You just need a starting point. One next step. One small promise kept to yourself. Change doesn't happen when you overhaul your entire life. It happens when you take one meaningful action and then another. That's it. That's the whole secret.

So choose your first step, and make it tiny. The power is not in doing it all—it's in getting started. Tiny steps signal something powerful to your brain: *I am doing this. I am capable of change. I follow through.* And once that identity starts to take root, everything else becomes easier. You begin to trust your decisions. You start protecting your time more fiercely. You feel more grounded walking into the classroom each morning.

222

Conclusion: This Is Your Moment

You show up with more energy for your students, your colleagues, and yourself. Because the truth is, when teachers feel supported, organized, and aligned, teaching becomes lighter. Not easy—but lighter. And that's the goal.

The work you're doing is brave. It's vulnerable. It's countercultural in a profession that still praises burnout as dedication. But you're not doing it alone. There are thousands of teachers who are rewriting the rules right alongside you. Even if you don't see it at your school, there are teachers who are choosing boundaries, choosing intention, choosing presence, and choosing joy. The Real Teacher Talk stories you've read throughout this book are proof of what's possible. Teachers just like you have transformed the way they teach, the way they organize, the way they think, and the way they care for themselves. And if they can do it in real classrooms with real kids and real demands, you can too.

Imagine what would be possible if more teachers stepped into this kind of empowerment. Imagine staff meetings filled with people who feel rested. Hallways where teachers don't avoid eye contact because they're drowning. Classrooms where kids are getting the best version of an adult who is actually resourced and supported. That vision isn't unrealistic. It starts with teachers like you who are willing to try something new. It starts with one small shift, one boundary, one system, one clarified priority. Those small shifts create ripples—ripples that change classrooms, teams, schools, and eventually, the culture of teaching itself.

If you're reading this and thinking, *I want support as I do this*, I want you to know that you don't have to figure it out alone. The Organized Teacher Club was created for teachers who want ongoing guidance, realistic strategies, and a supportive community as they implement The Organized Teacher System in real classrooms with real constraints. Inside OTC, you'll find step-by-step trainings, ready-to-use templates, monthly focus areas, and encouragement from teachers who are walking the same path. It's a place to return to when the year gets heavy, when systems need adjusting, or when you need a reminder that this work is possible and worth it. If this book resonated with you, OTC is simply the next place to put it into practice—at a pace that honors your life, your energy, and your season.

I wrote this book with a simple hope: that it becomes a soft place to land on the hard days and a spark of courage on the hopeful ones. You deserve a life that feels manageable. A workday that has a finish line. A classroom that feels calm and grounded.

223

Conclusion: This Is Your Moment

A sense of pride, not because you're overworked, but because you're aligned with what matters. So here is your invitation: take the next step today, even if it's small. Heck, especially if it's small.

You don't need to wait for the perfect moment. You don't need to wait for a new school year, a new administrator, or a different grade level. You don't need the system to change before you do. You can start right now, with whatever you have, exactly where you are.

And when you do, you will look back and realize this was the turning point. This was the moment you stopped surviving teaching and started shaping it—on your terms, in your voice, with your joy. You are an organized teacher. Not because your classroom is perfect or your inbox is empty, but because you are choosing to teach with intention. You've got this. And I'm cheering you on—today, tomorrow, and in every season that follows.

Teaching will never be perfect. There will be days when you feel like you have everything running smoothly and days when the systems slip and the paper piles return. That does not mean you have failed. It simply means you are human and you are learning. The key is not to stay stuck in those old habits, but to notice when it happens and gently guide yourself back to the systems that serve you.

Remember, your work is not only about checklists, timers, or organized trays. It is also about joy. Schedule time for fun, both in and out of the classroom. Laugh with your students. Celebrate small wins like a smooth transition, a parent who sends a kind note, or a student who finally remembered to write their name on the paper. And celebrate yourself too. Every time you show up and do your best, even when you feel tired or overwhelmed, you are making a difference.

When you feel discouraged, return to these pages. Pick one system, one routine, or one boundary that will make tomorrow just a little easier. Teaching is a journey, not a finish line. You will grow stronger and more confident with each season, and with every adjustment you make.

224

Conclusion: This Is Your Moment

Writing this book has been one of the most challenging and meaningful experiences of my education career so far, and it simply wouldn't exist without the people who supported me along the way. Completing this book while navigating prolonged legal proceedings often felt impossible, and there were days when continuing at all felt like a sheer act of persistence. I am profoundly grateful for everyone who helped me keep going.

To my sweet babies, Liv and Kai—you are my reason for everything. Thank you for reminding me to slow down and be silly and letting me be your mama. It's been the greatest gift of my life.

To my parents—thank you for instilling in me the belief that hard things are "figureoutable" and that showing up with integrity always matters. Your steady support carried me through the hardest chapters, both on and off the page.

To the teachers who have invited me into your classrooms, your inboxes, and your hearts over the years—this book is for you. Thank you for trusting me, for sharing your struggles and your wins, and for reminding me again and again why this work matters. Your willingness to try something new, even when you're exhausted, is the reason The Organized Teacher System exists.

To the incredible members of The Organized Teacher Club—your feedback, questions, and stories shaped so much of what ended up in these pages. You are the heartbeat of this work, and I am endlessly grateful for the way you show up for yourselves and for each other.

To Team Easy Teaching Tools—thank you for bringing this vision to life with me. To Jen, thank you for keeping our world organized, for clearing space on my calendar so I could write, and for caring about teachers as deeply as I do. To Sabrena, thank you for your creativity, your heart, and the way you connect our community with such authenticity. To Deba, thank you for your quiet brilliance behind the scenes and for making sure all the moving pieces actually *move*. To Alyssa, thank you for creating meaningful resources that make the lives of so many teachers easier. To this amazing team, your dedication and shared belief in this work made it possible for me to step back and pour fully into these pages.

To my editors and the entire team at Jossey-Bass—thank you for believing in this project from day one and for guiding me with lots of patience, clarity, and genuine care. Your expertise elevated this book in every possible way. And Sam and Christine, thank you for your patience and understanding when staying in integrity and meeting deadlines wasn't always feasible in this season of life.

To my friends who listened to brainstorms, drafts, tears, and "Is this chapter even good?" voice notes—thank you for keeping me grounded and cheering me on (especially Sol) when the writing felt impossible. You reminded me to rest, to breathe, and to keep going.

And finally, to every teacher picking up this book—thank you for the work you do each day. Thank you for being brave enough to protect your time, kind enough to care deeply, and wise enough to know you deserve support too. I hope these pages remind you of your strength and bring more ease, joy, and possibility into your teaching life.

About the Author

Kristen Donegan is an education professional with over 20 years of experience, including 13 years as an elementary teacher, a single mama of two, and a classroom efficiency ninja! Since 2010, she's been helping teachers just like you implement practical classroom hacks to save time, get organized, and finally find that magical thing called work/life balance.

Through her website Easy Teaching Tools, her Real Teacher Talk podcast, and her time-saving resources, Kristen supports thousands of teachers around the world. She also presents at professional development conferences and schools nationwide and leads popular programs like Easy Organization Tools and The Organized Teacher Club to help teachers make life in—and out of—the classroom a whole lot easier.

Printed and bound by CPI Group (UK) Ltd, Croydon, CR0 4YY

09/07/2026

14917364-0001